Cambridge Elements ☰

Elements in Public and Nonprofit Administration
edited by
Andrew Whitford
University of Georgia
Robert Christensen
Brigham Young University

RAGE GIVING

Jennifer A. Taylor
James Madison University
Katrina Miller-Stevens
Colorado College

CAMBRIDGE
UNIVERSITY PRESS

University Printing House, Cambridge CB2 8BS, United Kingdom

One Liberty Plaza, 20th Floor, New York, NY 10006, USA

477 Williamstown Road, Port Melbourne, VIC 3207, Australia

314–321, 3rd Floor, Plot 3, Splendor Forum, Jasola District Centre, New Delhi – 110025, India

103 Penang Road, #05–06/07, Visioncrest Commercial, Singapore 238467

Cambridge University Press is part of the University of Cambridge.

It furthers the University's mission by disseminating knowledge in the pursuit of education, learning, and research at the highest international levels of excellence.

www.cambridge.org
Information on this title: www.cambridge.org/9781108949873
DOI: 10.1017/9781108951036

© Jennifer A. Taylor and Katrina Miller-Stevens 2022

First published 2022

A catalogue record for this publication is available from the British Library.

ISBN 978-1-108-94987-3 Paperback
ISSN 2515-4303 (online)
ISSN 2515-429X (print)

Rage Giving

Elements in Public and Nonprofit Administration

DOI: 10.1017/9781108951036
First published online: April 2022

Jennifer A. Taylor
James Madison University

Katrina Miller-Stevens
Colorado College

Author for correspondence: Jennifer A. Taylor, Taylo2ja@jmu.edu

Abstract: After the 2016 election upheaval and polarized public discourse in the United States and the rise of radical-right and populist parties across the globe, a new phenomenon in online charitable giving has emerged – donating motivated by rage. This Element defines this phenomenon and discusses its meaning amidst the current body of research and knowledge on emotions and charitable giving, the implications of viral fundraising and increased social media use by both donors and nonprofit organizations, the intersectionality of rage giving and its meaning for practitioners and nonprofit organizations, the understanding of giving as a form of civic engagement, and the exploration of philanthropy as a tool for social movements and social change. Previous research shows contextual variation in charitable giving motivations; however, giving motivated by feelings of anger and rage is an unstudied behavioral shift in online giving.

Keywords: philanthropy, nonprofit, charitable giving, social movement, civic engagement

ISBNs: 9781108949873 (PB), 9781108951036 (OC)
ISSNs: 2515-4303 (online), 2515-429X (print)

Contents

1 Introduction to Rage Giving and Anger

It is clear that the political and social landscape has changed, with escalating globalization and political polarization. Not only are we contending with fake news infused into the political process, but unlike any president in the USA before him, there is an unfettered amount of declarations from the now-former "Tweeter-in-chief" (Anderson, 2017). Simultaneously, we have witnessed a surge in social media use (Smith & Anderson, 2018), and an undercurrent of anger and disbelief is employed to rally the polarized base. For example, the 2016 and 2020 US presidential elections were overwhelmingly emotionally charged and actively engaged elections with record voter turnout (Collinson, 2016; File, 2017; McDonald, 2020). In 2020, the percentage of voter eligible population rose to 66.7 percent, the highest on record since 1900 (McDonald, 2020). The public discourse has closely followed this surge in electoral activity of the radical right, observing that populist waves have also contributed to electoral upheaval in Brazil, Italy, and Mexico. This populist wave has added to the new landscape, igniting a fire of anger and protest and the emergence of a different kind of philanthropic impulse: rage giving.

The "fury triggers" have been described as "many and unending" that the feeling of anger grows and never goes away (McHugh, 2018). When more fuel is added to the fire, the rage intensifies. When the pent-up emotions burn out of control, rage givers experience an emotional release by channeling that rage into something positive (McHugh, 2018). While rage giving appears to be novel, channeling negative energy into decisive action is not new (McHugh, 2018). Previous studies linking negative emotions to giving reference the behavior as "civic anger," which relates charitable giving to targeted issues resulting from government actions and politics (Silber, 2012). Civic anger manifests in charitable giving due to individuals' dissatisfaction with events, politics, and policies in the public sphere (Silber, 2012). Other scholars refer to these emotions and movements as "empathic anger" that motivate people to counter injustice. Individuals experiencing empathic anger often associate feelings of altruism with higher levels of humanitarian concern for others, increased advocacy for social justice issues, increased tolerance for others, and an inclusive approach to civic engagement (Bringle, Hedgepath, & Wall, 2018). Empathetic anger can be a source of advocacy, civic engagement, and other prosocial behaviors.

The relationship between anger and emotion is connected to political mobilization. Anger and outrage are used as tools to provoke mobilization, action, and voting (Ost, 2004). In some examples, anger and outrage trigger precise emotions and, for a short time, inspire altruistic behaviors (Valentino et al., 2011), including rage giving.

Closely tied to feelings about the everyday policies, events, and activities in the public sphere, it is hard to pinpoint the first incident of rage giving. Once the website, ragedonate.com, was created, the pace of the trending hashtag #rageagainsthate quickly escalated (Lee, 2018). "RageDonate harnesses the power of that anger to deliver real change. If words and actions make your blood boil, click to donate to a cause that directly benefits those under threat. It feels good, and it does good" (Rage Donate, 2017). Americans were motivated to give money to those organizations that shared missions in sharp contrast to President Trump's policies. These included but were not limited to Planned Parenthood, the American Civil Liberties Union (ACLU), the Islamic Council on Foreign Relations, and the National Association for the Advancement of Colored People, among others (Mettler, 2016; Rinkunas, 2016).

This polarization in society produced many news articles and blogs about giving ignited by rage. Some of the articles focused on the strategies nonprofit organizations could employ to plan for and facilitate rage giving as a fundraising tool (Segedin, 2018), including tips for turning anger into action (Teson, 2017). Logically, the interest in this phenomenon makes sense because, within days after the 2016 US presidential election, Planned Parenthood received almost 80,000 donations. After President Trump's inauguration in 2017 and in response to several early official actions, the ACLU received more than $24 million in online donations (MacLaughlin, 2017). See Table 1 for a summary of the contributions these high-profile nonprofit organizations received during this time.

The emotional utility involved in rage giving is multifaceted serving several needs: political protest, altruism, and self-healing. Many charitable gifts were also made "in honor of" conservative politicians in the USA, many of which

Table 1 Rage giving leaderboard

Nonprofit Organization	Amount Raised (USD)	Number of Donors	Timeframe
American Civil Liberties Union	24 million	356,306	1 week
March for Our Lives	2.7 million	–	1 week
National Rifle Association	2.4 million	–	1 month
Planned Parenthood	–	315,000	1 month
Refugee and Immigrant Center for Education and Legal Services	20.7 million	553,000	1 week

Source: Data collected from various new articles cited in this manuscript.

produced an acknowledgment sent from the receiving NGO to the elected official (Mettler, 2016). Rage giving easily supported established nonprofit organizations that were ready to receive donations and were natural outlets for receiving rage gifts, thus producing an emotional release for donors. However, nonprofit organizations not equipped for this volume of individual giving were quickly overwhelmed. Dalia Fisch, a self-identified rage donor as quoted by Jessica Guynn (2018) in *USA Today*, states, "these small acts of armchair resistance are a release valve for pent-up feelings of helplessness, despair, and fury with the Trump administration . . . I find sadness debilitating. It doesn't help anyone. But giving really does. It takes away that powerlessness . . . all I recognize is that each time I get mad, I do it again" (paragraph 2). This anecdote mirrors the Geneva Emotion Wheel discussed in Section 4.4, wherein the axes are positive versus negative emotions and controlled versus uncontrolled (Scherer, 2005). The motivation for rage giving is inspired by concern for others (Hinde & Groebel, 1991). The investigation of rage giving represents a significant opportunity to consider social movements, activism, and giving behavior as interrelated. However, before the discussion on rage giving can begin, the emotions and anger that drive rage giving should be considered.

1.1 Types of Anger and Rage Giving

Emotions have been documented as a motivator for social movements and civic engagement, often rooted in empathy or sadness that creates a desire to help others (Bringle, Hedgepath, & Wall, 2018). Empathy comes in many forms, including distress, guilt, injustice, and anger. Prosocial responses from "empathic anger" often result in individuals taking action to help others who have suffered or experienced unjust circumstances (Vitaglione & Barnett, 2003; Hoffman, 2010; Bringle, Hedgepath, & Wall, 2018). Relatedly, "moral anger" is an emotional response to the injustice often felt by the individual experiencing unfair treatment. Within this vein, "civic anger" is "experienced by highly privileged subjects who witness the plight of others but are not themselves the primary object of unfair treatment" (Silber, 2012, p. 326).

The American Psychological Association (APA) distinguishes the emotions of anger and rage. Anger is "an emotion characterized by tension and hostility arising from frustration, real or imagined injury by another, or perceived injustice," whereas rage is an emotion characterized by "intense, typically uncontrolled anger . . . differentiated from hostility in that it is not necessarily accompanied by destructive actions but rather by excessive expressions" (APA, 2020). People experience emotions in different levels of intensity, as shown in Scherer (2005) and Plutchik's (2001) illustrations using a wheel-shaped color-coded figure and a flower-shaped color-coded figure to depict pleasant and unpleasant emotions. In each illustration, pleasant emotions are presented in cool colors of orange, yellow, and green and include love, relief, admiration, and joy, among others. Unpleasant emotions are presented in blue, purple, and red and include guilt, shame, disappointment, and fear, among others (Plutchik, 2001; Scherer, 2005). For both, the most unpleasant emotions are depicted in a bright red color to represent the highest intensity of all emotions. For the wheel-shaped illustration, the most intense red-colored emotion is anger. In the flower-shaped illustration, the most intense red-colored emotion is rage, which closely follows anger in the same petal of the flower.

According to Langstraat and Bowdon (2011), empathy and compassion are separate emotions that are often thought of as one. While someone may feel the empathy of an individual's experiences, compassion takes these feelings and adds a component of action. One who feels compassion not only feels terrible for an unfair situation but also takes effort to change the injustice. Compassion extends beyond the individual and is felt for multiple individuals who are suffering. It often connects individuals with others with shared social and political values (Nussbaum, 2001). Compassion can, however, have a negative result in that it creates power dynamics between "those who suffer and those who feel compassion, and the question of whether the actions borne from compassion can effectively lead to social justice" (Langstraat & Bowdon, 2011, p. 7).

Empathic anger may also trigger actions and responses that are directly related to emotion. In one study by Vitaglione and Barnett (2003), empathic anger is found to increase the need to help victims and punish those who harmed them. In this context, empathic anger mobilizes individuals to respond to injustice, and these responses can be both positive and negative. In a study by Bringle, Hedgepath, and Wall (2018), empathic anger is found to indicate higher degrees of altruism and humanitarian concern for others, more significant concerns for advocacy and social justice issues, more acceptance and non-prejudicial attitudes toward others, and a more inclusive approach to civic engagement (pp. 9–10). They conclude that empathic anger motivates individuals to take action and engage in community service and civic engagement. This type of motivation can result in rage giving as an emotional response in the form of anger that emerges from experience with politics or the political climate (McHugh, 2018; Taylor et al., 2018). In these instances, gifts are monetary and are often to nonprofit organizations directly impacted by the controversial issues related to politics or the political climate.

With the recent wave of political discontent and the emotional tides of the rising and falling political climate, it is becoming more critical than ever to understand the emotion of anger and its connection to rage givers. As such, throughout this Element, results of research conducted to explore individuals who donated to a charitable organization as an emotional response to the political climate of the presidential election of 2016 in the USA are presented to illustrate various points and observations of rage giving. The results are derived from a cross-sectional web survey of an online consumer panel sent to participants in 2017 with a focus on the two years around the 2016 presidential election. To participate, respondents needed to be eighteen years of age or older during the 2016 presidential election. The entry question to the survey asked participants, "Did you donate to a nonprofit organization or policy advocacy organization in the last 24 months (2 years) in protest of the political climate, public policy, or elected or appointed government officials?" If a respondent answered yes, participants continued with the survey. If the respondent answered no, the survey ended.

Questions in the instrument were modeled after previously administered surveys measuring individuals' attitudes toward donating online (Treiblmaier & Pollach, 2006), emotional uplift (Bennett, 2009), emotional utility (Sargeant, Ford, & West, 2006), behavioral anger responses (Linden et al., 2003; Miers et al., 2007), social media intensity and influence (Ellison, Steinfield, & Lampe, 2007), and levels of civic engagement attitudes and behaviors (Doolittle & Faul, 2013) to increase the validity of the survey. Five hundred and fifty-one surveys were completed in a random sample of individuals from across the United States, 520 of which are usable for this research. The study results are discussed throughout the following sections, but the demographics of the sample are presented here.

1.2 Who Participates in Rage Giving?

As noted previously, all individuals in the sample presented in this research have indicated they donated to a nonprofit organization or policy advocacy organization in the two years surrounding the 2016 presidential election in protest of the political climate, public policy, or elected or appointed government officials. Table 2 illustrates the demographic makeup of the sample of 520 respondents. As shown, the sample is skewed heavily in the category of ethnicity with 80% of respondents reporting White ($n = 417$) with the next largest category being Black or African American at 6% ($n = 32$) closely followed by Hispanic/Latino/Spanish origin ($n = 31$) and Asian ($\underline{n} = 23$). We discuss the skewed ethnicity toward White individuals and other limitations in this sample,

Table 2 Demographic statistics of the sample of rage givers (n = 520)

Characteristic	*n*	Characteristic	*n*
Party Affiliation		Education	
Republican	128	Some high school	9
Democrat	229	High school graduate or equivalent	63
Independent	146	Some college credit or no degree	111
Other	17	Trade/technical/vocational	15
		Associate's degree	57
Gender		Bachelor's degree	159
Female	300	Master's degree	76
Male	215	Professional degree (MD, JD, or DDS)	21
Trans female/woman	1	Doctorate degree	9
Genderqueer/gender nonconforming	4		
		Ethnicity	
Age		White	417
18–29	125	Hispanic, Latino, or Spanish	31
30–39	101	Black or African American	32
40–49	70	American Indian or Alaska Native	5
50–59	67	Asian	23
60–69	106	Middle Eastern or North African	1
70–79	47	Native Hawaiian/Pacific Islander	3
80+	4	Other	8
Employment Status		Annual Household Income	
Full-time work	250	Less than $50,000	163
Part-time work	73	$50,000–$74,999	126
Unemployed	27	$75,000–$99,999	104
Retired	118	$100,000–$149,999	81
Student full-time	13	$150,000–$199,999	23
Stay-at-home parent	30	$200,000–$249,000	14
Other	9	$250,000 or over	9

in the intersectionality of rage giving section of this Element. The remaining categories of ethnicity are in the single digits. Gender is more evenly distributed with 58% (*n* = 300) of respondents reporting female and 41% (*n* = 215) reporting male. Five respondents reported either trans female or genderqueer/ gender nonconforming.

Education shows variation across categories, but more than half of respondents have an undergraduate degree or a graduate degree (51 percent, $n = 265$). The two individual categories with the most responses are bachelor's degrees ($n = 150$) and some college but not a degree ($n = 111$). This is followed by respondents with master's degrees ($n = 71$), high school graduates ($n = 63$), and associate degrees ($n = 57$). The remaining categories of some high school, doctoral degrees, and professional degrees have 21 respondents or less.

The age of respondents is distributed across categories, with the three most prominent groups being individuals between the ages of 18 and 29 (24%, $n = 125$), 30 and 39 (19%, $n = 101$), and 60 and 69 (20%, $n = 106$). Middle-aged individuals make up a quarter of the respondents, with 26% of individuals being between the ages of 40 and 59. Almost half of the respondents (48%, $n = 250$) are engaged in full-time employment, with the next largest group being retired individuals (27%, $n = 118$). Part-time workers made up 14% of respondents ($n = 73$), with the remaining categories as 5% or less of respondents. Two-thirds of respondents ($n = 393$) report an annual household income of $99,999 or below, with the most respondents coming from annual household incomes of less than $50,000 ($n = 162$). Party affiliation is made up of 44% ($n = 229$) Democrats, 25% ($n = 128$) Republicans, and 28% ($n = 146$) Independents. In part, the results and examples presented in this Element are based on the previously mentioned sample of rage givers. We recognize the sample is skewed, and there are limitations in what we can glean from this particular group of respondents. Regardless, a sample of this size ($n = 520$ respondents) also offers insights into the topic of rage giving that are useful and thought-provoking and advance our knowledge and research in this area.

1.3 Summary

The study of rage giving is essential in that it enhances our understanding of behavioral shifts and motivations related to giving as an emotional response to anger. The 2016 presidential election provides a platform to illustrate the emotional investment and action-oriented response of rage donors while also shedding light on a new type of viral activism. Understanding rage giving will help researchers and practitioners in nonprofit organizations ascertain how to appeal to and motivate individuals to donate online out of sentiment and behavioral responses to political and social injustices.

In the following sections, this Element fills the gap in the giving and philanthropy literature by exploring all aspects of rage giving, from the individual emotions of anger to the online venues that provide the platform for this type of giving. Section 2 provides an overview of rage giving as it relates to political movements and civic engagement. Section 3 explains the significant trends in social media and viral fundraising that helped rage giving make its mark on philanthropy. Section 4 looks more closely at the intersectionality of rage givers and the characteristics that make up this group of individuals beyond basic demographics. The last section, Section 5, concludes with suggestions for nonprofit practitioners and organizations that may be interested in adopting rage giving as a tool for fundraising, emphasizing both the positive and negative aspects of this fundraising strategy.

2 Political Movements and Civic Engagement

Anger is often a central part of politics and political action. Emotion is used as a tool to motivate individuals to participate in social movements, civic engagement, and political advocacy (Ost, 2004; Ford et al., 2019). Anger can be interpreted as a form of communication as ideas, thoughts, and concerns are expressed through protest marches and speeches or by smaller actions such as bumper stickers on cars or donating to nonprofit organizations (Valentino et al., 2011). Expressions of anger can create public dialogue on social and political injustices, and in many ways, feelings of anger are used to transform wrongdoings into good deeds (Lyman, 2004; Cantrell, 2019).

Individuals who feel disrupted in their lives or threatened by politicians or political climates may often feel a mix of anger, concern, fear, or distress, and it is these emotions that motivate and provide a reason for people to act (Woods et al., 2012). In short, political participation and emotions of anger may go hand in hand, and anger can transform a passive citizen into an engaged protestor. If individuals are angry, they are more likely to take action and participate in protests or other forms of civic engagement, political advocacy, and social action (Valentino et al., 2011; Mayer, 2020).

This cause-and-effect connection between anger and action can also be linked to political mobilization. As Ost (2004) notes, "anger is built into politics through the everyday activities of political parties, which continually both stoke and mobilize anger in order to gain and maintain support" (p. 230). Political climates, and some political candidates, in particular, trigger specific emotions in individuals that may motivate individuals to take philanthropic action (Valentino et al., 2011; Valentino, Wayne, & Oceno, 2018), one form of which is rage giving. This section starts with a discussion of individual motivators for action to help contextualize this link between anger, political and social movements, and civic engagement.

2.1 Individual Motivators for Action

When thinking of the role of anger within philanthropy, charitable giving, and social capital, one can posit that an individual participating in rage giving may be doing so as a result of their interests in the collective good or community. In many ways, rage giving facilitates its collective action and social capital among those who are disgruntled with the political climate (Coleman, 1988). The connection between rage giving and social capital supports the tenets of critical emotion studies in that rage giving is a thought-out behavior in response to an emotion, and the response itself is social or cultural in nature. Critical emotion studies argue that rather than thinking of emotions as void of reason or thought, emotion and thought are actually connected. Emotions create awareness and help us think analytically and critically, and they often inform our motivations and intentions (Gilbert, 2017). While emotions appear to be individual responses, they are often informed by "emotional rules that are negotiated by groups and enforced by individuals and groups" (Winans, 2012, p. 155). Emotions inform our attention and awareness of issues, and they form our judgments of what to do in response to those issues (Micciche, 2007).

Actions taken to donate in response to the political climate, founded in emotions of anger or rage, are driven from the climate one observes or the social movements one wants to be a part of, as illustrated in Figure 1. This type of donation is often given to a nonprofit organization that is directly impacted by controversial issues related to politics, social justice, or public policy. As Bringle, Hedgepath, and Wall (2018) note, empathic anger indicates higher degrees of altruism and humanitarian concern for others, greater concerns for advocacy and social justice issues, more acceptance and non-prejudicial attitudes toward others, and a more inclusive approach to civic engagement (pp. 9–10). They conclude that empathic anger motivates individuals to take action and engage in community service. It is this collective action that may provide an individual the satisfaction of changing an undesirable situation or merely giving that individual a method to express their displeasure (Gamson & Meyer, 1996; Greenaway et al., 2016).

Rage giving is an emotional response to anger that may emerge from an individual's experience with politics or the political climate (McHugh, 2018; Taylor et al., 2018). One interpretation of this response is in the form of civic anger, which links philanthropic giving to targeted issues resulting from government actions and politics (Silber, 2012). Civic anger is "experienced by

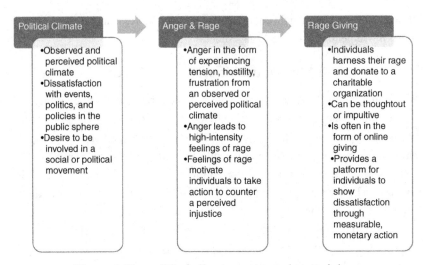

Figure 1 The political climate, anger, and rage giving

highly privileged subjects who witness the plight of others but are not them-selves the primary object of unfair treatment" (Silber, 2012, p. 326). Civic anger relies on challenging the government to make improvements by relying on the political discontent of individuals who can donate and participate in philan-thropic protests. For example, in 2012, Jewish philanthropists in Israel partici-pated in civic anger as a way to express their displeasure at governmental incompetency, irresponsibility, and the "realm of politics as such" (Silber, 2012, p. 325).

Giving as an emotional release to anger is considered a prosocial behavior in that its purpose is to benefit or help others in need. Prosocial behaviors are defined as altruistic behaviors or "the desire to expend efforts to benefit other people" through voluntary acts without expecting anything in return (Grant, 2008, p. 49; Perry, Hondeghem, & Wise, 2010). Examples include helping a neighbor, volunteering for a nonprofit organization, serving on a nonprofit board, or engaging with policy advocacy or community activities. The benefit of helping others provides the individual motivation to give, and in many cases, positive psychological benefits result from these actions (Bekkers & Wiepking, 2007). Prosocial behaviors are often shaped by an individual's experiences, ideologies, and communities (Rainey & Steinbauer, 1999; Ward & Miller-Stevens, 2020).

Prosocial behaviors are "other-oriented," in contrast to an individual's self-interest. Philosophers, economists, and social psychologists have an ongoing debate concerning the core motivations of these helping behaviors: truly altru-istic, without the expectation of reciprocity, or self-interested. Batson (2012) defines prosocial behaviors as "the broad range of actions intended to benefit one or more people other than oneself – behaviors such as helping, comforting, sharing, and cooperation, philanthropy, and community service" (p. 243). Prosocial behaviors are characterized by a concern for the rights, feelings, and welfare of other people (Vitaglione & Barnett, 2003; Hoffman, 2010; Bellucci et al., 2020). Behaviors that can be characterized as prosocial include feeling empathy and concern for others and actively acting in ways to help or benefit other people through civic and community engagement (e.g. giving, volunteering, voting, policy advocacy; Grant, 2008).

Prosocial orientations of individuals encourage private action for the public good in both laboratory experiments and individuals' stated intention to participate in collective action like voting and contributing to other public goods (Jankowski, 2002, 2007; Edlin, Gelman, & Kaplan, 2007; Fowler & Kam, 2007; Dawes, Loewen, & Fowler, 2011; Bellucci et al., 2020). These behaviors build an individual's "networks, norms, and social trust that facilitate coordination and cooperation for mutual benefits" (Putnam, 1995, p. 67). They can be measured by "a combination of a number of connections and societal involvements, reciprocity of those relationships, political participation, and attitudes and perceptions of the local community" (Brown & Ferris, 2007; Yao, 2015, p. 8).

This line of inquiry suggests that individuals are predisposed to acting prosocially and also to engaging in their communities. As such, their socialization practices, institutions with which they engage, events they experience, and ideologies shape the "general, altruistic motivation to serve the interests of a community of people, a state, a nation or humankind" (Rainey & Steinbauer, 1999, p. 20). With this in mind, we turn to one manifestation of prosocial behaviors in the form of civic engagement as it relates to rage giving.

2.2 Civic Engagement and Rage Giving

The United States can be thought of as a large fabric of individuals that comprise a patchwork of different communities. Political messages in recent years have broken, rather than rebuilt, this community, and where there were deep chasms of discontent and distrust, the desire for social and political change fueled by furious triggers and intensified rage has led to the operationalization of that anger and emotion into charitable giving and volunteering (Rage Donate, 2017). This collective wave of giving for good is the embodiment of civic engagement embedded in relationships in the public sphere for the purpose of facilitating social or collective action (Coleman, 1988; Wray-Lake et al., 2019).

Civic engagement is defined as "the process of believing that one can and should make a difference in enhancing his or her community" and includes both civic engagement attitudes and civic engagement behaviors (Doolittle & Faul, 2013, p. 2). Civic engagement attitudes are the beliefs and feelings of an individual toward his or her community and the impacts that individuals can make on the community (p. 2). Civic engagement behaviors are the actions individuals take to make those impacts happen (p. 2). As illustrated in Putnam's influential work (2000), levels of civic engagement can be positively affected by war, depression, and natural disasters as shown after the terrorist attacks of September 11, 2001, on the United States, during which civic engagement significantly increased across all ethnic groups, social classes, religions, genders, and ages. More recently, the Black Lives Matter movement has emerged as a civic engagement and social movement response to the "state-sanctioned murders of several unarmed Black Americans" (Tanksley, 2019, p. ii). After witnessing such events as national tragedies and unjust murders, Americans are more likely to attend political meetings, participate in community events and marches, and have an interest in current affairs (Putnam, 2002; Robinson, 2019).

The sentiment that national tragedies are a catalyst for civic engagement also applies to America's political climate and the 2016 presidential election, where individuals responded en masse to protest newly elected President Trump's victory and, conversely, where President Trump's supporters marched in celebration. Before Trump's victory, one reporter noted, "With the outsized victories of outliers Donald Trump and Bernie Sanders in the New Hampshire primary, the essence of 2016 becomes clear: this election is about anger. Trump is riding a wave of dangerous xenophobia anger among Republicans, while Sanders is riding a wave of righteous anger among Democrats at a 'rigged economy'" (Seaquist, 2017). The increase in civic engagement attitudes and beliefs was palpable during the time of this election.

Since the 2016 election, surveys exploring the level of happiness in America, level of optimism for the future, and satisfaction with "the way things are going" have shown a clear bifurcation between individuals associated with the Democratic, Republican, and Independent parties (Graham & Pinto, 2017; Swift, 2016). In surveys by Swift (2016) and Graham and Pinto (2017), Democrats and Independents were shown to experience significant drops in their level of satisfaction with America, whereas Republicans' satisfaction remained stable. Conversely, Republicans' optimism toward the future increased after the 2016 election, while that of Democrats and Independents decreased. These results are reflected in the civic engagement efforts of individuals who participate in giving to nonprofit organizations and organize marches or other civic engagement activities that express a voice of discontent. Examples include the Women's Marches across the United States after Donald Trump was elected to office and the plethora of donations made during and after the election to organizations such as Planned Parenthood, the ACLU, the Islamic Council on Foreign Relations, and the National Association for the Advancement of Colored People, among others (Mettler, 2016; Rinkunas, 2016; Nicolaou & Smith, 2019).

When viewing civic engagement and anger through the lens of political affiliation, individuals who are engaged in political participation beyond voting tend to strongly identify with their political party and are more civically engaged (Groenendyk & Banks, 2014). These individuals are also angrier, and this anger is viewed as a modifier between party identification and civic engagement. This strong party identification is used to bring people together and to mobilize social movements (Groenendyk & Banks, 2014). In short, negative or dividing events create rallying points for individuals to protest the political climate through several different civic engagement behaviors, one of which is online donating in the form of rage giving.

Previous research has illustrated that emotions facilitate collective action and social capital among those who are disgruntled with the political climate (Coleman, 1988; Ford et al., 2019). Actions taken to donate or volunteer in response to the political climate, founded in emotions of anger or feelings of unrest, are driven from the climate one observes or the social movements one wants to be a part of. Rage giving provides a platform for these individuals to show their dissatisfaction through a measurable action illustrating their desire to improve the political climate while also relating to the collective good or community (Rage Donate, 2017; McHugh, 2018). With monetary donations to nonprofit organizations that either work on or are the target of political issues or social injustices, one can feel satisfied knowing they are contributing toward the change of an undesirable situation, or they are fulfilling the self-gratifying emotion of expressing their displeasure (Gamson & Meyer, 1996; Bennett & Gabriel, 1999). It is this emotional uplift that motivates to give and participate in civic engagement activities.

As noted in the introduction, emotions are a motivator for social movements and civic engagement that are often rooted in empathy that fosters a desire to help others (Bringle, Hedgepath, & Wall, 2018). Empathy is illustrated and described as distress, guilt, injustice, and anger (Bringle, Hedgepath, & Wall, 2018). Empathic anger can result in individuals taking action to help individuals who are suffering, damaged, or abused (Vitaglione & Barnett, 2003; Hoffman, 2010). Similarly, moral anger is a response to injustices felt by individuals experiencing unfair or unjust treatment.

Individuals who donate and volunteer do indeed believe they can make a difference in their communities. By donating and volunteering as an emotional response to the political climate, individuals are engaging in both civic engagement action and civic engagement behaviors. While a donation may be a small action in itself, the byproducts of that action can be a driving force of inspiration and motivation to other individuals and the nonprofit organization receiving the donation. In essence, individuals who donate believe they are making a difference and enhancing their community (Doolittle & Faul, 2013).

2.3 An Empirical Understanding of Rage Giving and Civic Engagement

In an attempt to better understand the connection between rage giving and civic engagement, Section 1 introduced a cross-sectional web survey conducted in 2017 that asked participants to respond to questions related to anger and levels of civic engagement attitudes and behaviors. To participate in the study, respondents had to have donated to a nonprofit organization or policy advocacy organization in the two years surrounding the 2016 presidential election as an action in protest of the political climate, public policy, or elected or appointed government officials. The survey was modeled after previous studies asking questions on the conceptual elements of attitudes toward donating online (Treiblmaier & Pollach, 2006), emotional uplift (Bennett, 2009), behavioral anger response (Linden et al., 2003; Miers et al., 2007), social media intensity and influence (Ellison, Steinfield, & Lampe, 2007), and levels of civic engagement attitudes and behaviors (Doolittle & Faul, 2013). Civic engagement was operationalized as civic engagement attitudes and civic engagement behaviors, with civic engagement attitudes including the beliefs and feelings of an individual toward his or her community and the impacts that individual can make on the community and civic engagement behaviors including the actions individuals take to make those impacts (Doolittle & Faul, 2013, p. 2). As noted in Section 1, 520 surveys were in the final data set. Demographics of this data are presented in the other chapters of this book.

The estimation and ordinary least squares (OLS) regression results showed a positive association between rage giving and civic engagement, indicating a relationship exists between the two concepts. Regression models illustrated that individuals who participate in rage giving and believe the action creates an emotional uplift also have increased civic engagement attitudes and behaviors. In contrast, those who avoid emotional feelings of anger tend to have decreased levels of civic engagement attitudes and behavior.

Also, individuals who think positively about online donating tend to have higher levels of civic engagement. Still, those who do not engage in social media activities have a lower level of civic engagement, indicating that online activity leads to more participation in civic engagement. The study also showed that civic engagement attitudes and behaviors of rage givers tend to increase with age and achieve education. Political affiliation resulted in more civic engagement behaviors in rage donors, but not civic engagement attitudes.

Using this same data set, Lee (2018) found a significant relationship between anger and political advocacy, a subset of civic engagement. When individuals are angry, they are more likely to respond through political advocacy, rather than not acting. This indicates that people's efforts to change social systems are related to their behavioral responses, especially anger. Also, an individual's civic engagement activities increase when that person is more interested and involved with political advocacy. Conversely, Lee (2018) found satisfaction with the political culture and political party affiliation not as impactful on an individual's civic engagement activities as on their political advocacy efforts. Lee concludes that behavior responses, including anger and civic engagement, do influence an individual's likeliness to rage donate.

In sum, it is evident that the relationship between anger and community engagement exists. Those who tend to be angry about a cause, social injustice, or political issue are more likely to engage in rage donating and are more likely to participate in other civic engagement activities. In short, anger creates an impetus and motivation for social movements and civic engagement.

2.4 Summary

Rage giving, as a paradigmatic shift in donor behavior, aligns with both prosocial behaviors and civic engagement by giving a voice to the underserved and unheard. Individuals who participate in rage giving do believe they can make a difference both in their communities and in the political sphere, and they believe their actions will bring about social and political change. Rage giving is not limited to a one-sided viewpoint, but rather the act of giving as an emotional response to anger can be in support or opposition to any cause, social injustice, or policy issue. Rage givers are Democrats, Republicans, and Independents alike. Regardless of political perspective, donors who participate in rage giving believe their donation will make an impact. Rage giving is a new form of philanthropy and a powerful tool of communication that creates collective action and increases civic engagement in times of despair or frustration.

3 Social Media and Fundraising

As discussed thus far, the rapid diffusion of the Internet in society and the adoption of communications and marketing strategies through social media by politics, government, and nonprofit organizations have enlarged and focused the landscape of the public sphere. These rapid changes in technology adoption and globalization have changed how systems, organizations, groups, and individuals work together to pursue the public interest. Most recently, the growing use of social media in nonprofit organizations has emerged as a niche research area (Namisango & Kang, 2018) and a necessary strategy in a new communication landscape (Kietzmann et al., 2011) for building sustainable organizations, with wide-ranging implications for organizational strategy and collective action.

The use of social media is inexpensive and can be an effective marketing strategy, especially if organizations embrace the shift to a dialogic approach. The value of the relationship between the individual and the public interest is based on iterative communication and value co-creation. The social media ecosystem is defined as "mobile and web-based technologies that create highly interactive platforms via which individuals and communities share, co-create, discuss, and modify user-generated content" (Kietzmann et al., 2011, p. 241).

Three major approaches define the changing expectations in marketing strategy: transactional, relational, and value co-creation (Prahalad & Ramaswamy, 2004; Ramaswamy & Ozcan, 2014; Taylor et al., 2018). Transactional exchange occurs when the value is exchanged between entities with no expectation of reciprocity, whereas in relational exchange, the value exchange exists between entities over time. Value co-creation as a strategic marketing paradigm originates in the customer's willingness to participate in creating a new product or service, representing an avenue to create a competitive advantage (Prahalad & Ramaswamy, 2004). This is especially true in rage giving, where nonprofit organizations can align their mission with a giving opportunity and civic engagement opportunities, reap the benefits of an expanded social and political capital network, and raise an extraordinary amount of financial support in the process. The act of making a rage gift places a donor in co-creation.

In the case of rage giving, most of the opportunities were not premeditated by the nonprofit organizations, except in the ACLU. During strategic planning sessions, ACLU staff modeled potential policy impacts of a Trump presidency based on his campaign rhetoric. ACLU staff developed marketing and communications plans to drive engagement with their mission and, subsequently, donations. Attaining a competitive advantage in the nonprofit sector necessitates the adoption of value co-creation as an organizational strategy.

By forecasting the political climate, aligning communications and solicitations of a charitable mission provides significant promise for the development of competitive advantage.

In the nonprofit sector, the shift to new paradigms happens more slowly, as most nonprofit organizations are risk-averse, under-resourced, and under-skilled in marketing and communications (Pope, Sterrett, & Asamoa-Tutu, 2009). Risk-taking is both theoretically and empirically connected with innovation (Miller, 1983; Covin & Slevin, 1998). Hull and Lio (2006) find that nonprofit organizations tend to be significantly more risk-averse, and thus less innovative, than other private or public organizations, due primarily to their complex governance structures and stakeholder accountabilities (Williams & Taylor, 2013).

Next, we present a brief review of social media use by nonprofit organizations and focus on a critical function in nonprofit organizations' social media use – that is, community engagement. Then, we highlight emerging research in online charitable giving and discuss the relationships of rage givers to social media and fundraising.

3.1 Social Media Use by Nonprofit Organizations

Recent survey findings report that social media adoption by nongovernmental organizations (NGOs) worldwide is extensive: "93% of NGOs have a Facebook Page, 77% have a Twitter Profile, 56% have a LinkedIn Page, and 50% have an Instagram Profile" (Nonprofit Tech for Good, 2018, p. 10). Additionally, the findings share that NGOs have significant bases of followers on social media, even in smaller NGOs. With communication and a support base, this substantial and new way for nonprofit organizations to communicate with the public, and the potential impact of a viral campaign, is significant. The Nonprofit Technology Network indicates that Twitter and Facebook have become integral communication tools that "supplement and supplant the traditional Website" (Nonprofit Technology Network, 2011, p. 2). The 2018 M+R Benchmarks Study provides further support for the widespread use and utility of digital interactions to drive nonprofit communications (~4.7 billion email messages), engagement (~527 thousand clicks through to websites), and subsequent support (~12 million donations) from a sample of 154 small, medium, and large nonprofit organizations (Nonprofit Technology Network, 2011).

The financial benefits of integrating social media as a primary function of an overall strategy for nonprofit organizations are plentiful. Suh (2020) finds that the financial stability of a nonprofit leads to more effective use of social media. Utilizing embedded networks of support on social media increases financial performance, reduces promotional expenses (Icha & Agwu, 2015; Rathi, Given, & Forcier, 2016), and increases charity brand awareness. However, many nonprofit organizations fail to realize the value of an integrated social media plan. In the rise of rage giving in early 2017, very few nonprofit organizations were able to predict the potential emotional response of supporters, even fewer were able to handle the onslaught of donations. Only one organization from the Rage Giving Leaderboard presented in Section 1 of this Element, indicated that the potential for rage giving was part of the communications, marketing, and, most importantly, fundraising strategy (Romero & Rozanski, 2017). The nonprofit sector trends a reactionary rather than a proactive approach in social media marketing with unarticulated goals and strategy (Thackeray et al., 2012; Adjei, Annor-Frempong, & Bosompem, 2016).

Nah and Saxton (2013) identify six functions of social media by nonprofit organizations: relationships, information exchange, conversation and interaction, co-creation and innovation, community building, and reputation and legitimacy. Several of these functions of social media use in the nonprofit sector undergird a broader marketing strategy, and community engagement is often unspecified. These organizations use social media as a marketing channel to tap into their networks of support to communicate needs, share information, rally advocates, and maintain relationships with supporters and allies.

3.2 Social Media as Community Engagement

Social media use by nonprofit organizations creates opportunities for engagement in networks to increase mission support in advocacy, charity brand awareness, and fundraising. As a principal community engagement strategy, its integration into marketing, communications, and fundraising plans strengthens its capacity to work with the community (Waters et al., 2009; Warner, Abel, & Hachtmann, 2014; Young, 2017) and broadens its network of support (Gálvez-Rodriguez, Caba-Perez, & Lopez-Godoy, 2014; Guidry et al., 2017). As discussed earlier, social media requires minimal investment with high returns (Rathi, Given, & Forcier, 2016). Due to its dialogic nature, it offers supporters the opportunity to co-create with missions that resonate.

The most immediate use of a new social media account with a nonprofit is to engage with its community (Waters et al., 2009; Warner, Abel, & Hachtmann, 2014; Young, 2017). Nonprofit organizations put up a page, haphazardly provide information on their mission, and then begin slowly to have conversations with supporters and build their network. The goals of community engagement strategies focus on solving community problems or issues and soliciting community input toward enhanced service design. Nonprofit organizations also rely on social media as a relationship-building strategy (Wyllie et al., 2016; Lai et al., 2017). They seek to build strong relationships with the community as a crucial component of their service delivery process. For example, Rocktown Rallies, in Harrisonburg, Virginia, is a group of volunteers who saw a need to increase their support for new immigrant families in their community. They set up a social media account, received donations in-kind and financial gifts, and quickly found themselves setting up a new legal structure, a 501(c)3 in the USA, to scale the organization and its impact. And while they have grown significantly, gaining legitimacy, they still solicit the loan of car seats, the gifts of linens, and potluck dinners from volunteers and donors to continue with their mission (J. Hulsey, personal communication, July 2019). In the process of growing, quite exponentially, Rocktown Rallies has discovered a new way to use social media as a path to organizational legitimacy (Feng, Du, & Ling, 2017; Young, 2017) while still crowdsourcing (car seats, potlucks, drivers, clothes, English lessons, etc.) for these new immigrant families. A few years into community engagement, crowdsourcing, as volunteers, they find themselves in the business of value co-creating for the nonprofit as needs arise. All of this affords them legitimacy as a nonprofit (Feng, Du, & Ling, 2017; Peng, 2017; Sorensen, Andrews, & Drennan, 2017; Young, 2017). Although nonprofit organizations acknowledge the value of social media, many remain unaware of the extensive opportunity embedded in social media.

Focusing on growing the human resource capacity in organizations, Cravens frames online volunteering (also known as *virtual volunteering, e-volunteering,* and *micro volunteering)* as "unpaid labor undertaken for the benefit of an NGO, charity, school, community organization, etc., or those served by such, where an online system (accessed through a computer, a mobile device, etc.) plays a key role in volunteer recruitment, in facilitating access to tasks, and in the volunteer conducting that task" (2014, p. 5). Volunteers who are active as online volunteers are also enthusiastic offline volunteers, suggesting that the venues of volunteering complement rather than compete with each other (Ihm, 2017). It is worth noting that with the generations of Generation X and Millennials, social media use, and its integration as part of their daily lives, is more prevalent than other generations.

Young (2017) advises nonprofit organizations to conduct a technology assessment and to employ three to five social media platforms and "employ it well," as opposed to operating on all of the platforms. Organizations should assess the capacity of the organization and staff, the market segmentation represented by and within different platforms, and how the use of social media aligns with organizational goals such as fundraising, information and awareness, programming, and service delivery, among others. Like other communication channels, it is important to develop a strategy to mobilize supporters who are active online volunteers and donors. Additional research is presented in Section 4 as we explore the intersecting identities of rage givers.

The existing literature on social media in nonprofit organizations signals the extent of social media use among these organizations. While Nah and Saxton (2013) present the functions of social media, they also include an analysis of the enablers and inhibitors of social media use. And in our results, we see that a few nonprofit organizations that were beneficiaries of rage giving have mastered these other functions with supporters. While nonprofit organizations may mainly seem to use social media for information sharing, community creation, and collective action, it is clear that other collaborative activities such as co-creation and giving behaviors also occur. However, few studies have explored these behaviors. In the rage giving data set presented in Sections 1 and 2, we explore the social media use, influence, and intensity and familiarity of donors with online giving.

3.3 Online Giving

Like market-based firms, the importance of online transactions, relational exchange, and, now, value co-creation has become a necessary strategy to competitive advantage. In the United States, online giving has risen for the last decade by 23 percent since 2017 (Nonprofit Source, 2018). Many factors have contributed to this growth, including the expansive integration of the Internet in daily life worldwide. Nonprofit Source (2018) shares a statistical compilation or dashboard of online giving worldwide. Globally, 54 percent of donors prefer to make donations with a credit card online with an average gift of $128. Giving Tuesday, a global initiative by the nonprofit sector to engage supporters during the holiday shopping season, raised $380 million in 2019, across more than 150 countries, and made 14.2 billion social media impressions. Fifty-five percent of supporters who engage with nonprofit organizations on social media take some type of action (advocacy, volunteering, or giving). More importantly, research demonstrates that the donor retention rate of online donors is more than 60 percent (Nonprofit Source, 2018). Monthly giving programs, text-to-give, and responsive website design have also contributed to the aggressive growth in online giving.

Facilitating the ease of giving and communicating social impact and need via digital strategies is the future of fundraising. However, online fundraising effectiveness and strategy have received little systematic treatment in the research literature. Thus far, research has been limited to anecdotal evidence, fundraisers' intuition, and advice from for-profit firms such as Blackbaud,

Salesforce, and smaller independent groups. Additionally, education at the university level has yet to include online communications competencies (Nonprofit Academic Centers Council, 2019; Network of Schools of Public Policy, Affairs, and Administration, n.d.).

Existing studies on online fundraising are limited in their design for several reasons: low N, nonrandom samples, quasi-experimental designs, substitution away from another channel, and unpredictable activity by supporters (Lewis & Reiley, 2014; Blake, Nosko, & Tadelis, 2015; Lewis & Rao, 2015). Participation is also subject to the broader cultural environment, as in the research discussed here. In a recent large experimental research design in Germany in partnership with the global NGO, Save the Children, results indicate extensive substituting among nonprofit organizations. This research provides further evidence that individuals' donation budgets may not be increasing (Thaler, 1985) and that online fundraising causes some redistribution of the marketing channel in which supporters give (Adena & Hager, 2020). However, the rapid increase in social media impressions, internet traffic, number of donors, and donor retention provide support for the "the power of asking" (Yörük, 2009; Andreoni & Rao, 2011) and for the old fundraising adage, "when you fail to ask, you fail to receive."

3.4 Rage Giving and Online Fundraising

Another factor to consider is presented in the context of rage giving: the volatility and complexity of viral marketing. Viral marketing, or viral advertising, is a marketing strategy that exploits existing social networks to promote a product or service. Similar to how a virus spreads in a community, viral marketing refers to how consumers spread information about a product or service with others (Helm, 2010). It combines traditional word of mouth or customer referral techniques and allows for rapid dissemination to millions of people in a short amount of time (Helm, 2010; Haryani & Motwani, 2015).

Predicting consumer responses in an uncontrolled environment is complex and can have unintended positive and negative consequences; it is a double-edged sword. Massive influxes of donations and visibility cause many nonprofit missions to buckle or collapse under the weight of so much goodwill, so fast. Viral campaigns can be premediated and orchestrated by professional staff or generate spontaneously within social networks. In 2014, the ALS Ice Bucket Challenge was initiated by a high-profile donor, spread through social networks; the organization seized the moment and capitalized on the phenomenon, raising $115 million in about two months, acquiring 739,000 new donors (Taylor & Noble, 2015; ALS Association, n.d.). Ultimately, the windfall had many positive effects, such as increasing the number of patients served by 28 percent, clearing the waitlist for power-assisted wheelchairs nationwide, and pouring $80 million into research, but the capacity of the nonprofit to meet its mission went unfulfilled (Piper, 2019). Five years later, the ALS Association is still running a tremendous annual budget deficit, trying to spend down the windfall of donations. Additional criticisms of the initial viral campaign, and the subsequent reboots, include the social pressure to individuals to do good publicly but not give, the pressure for nonprofit organizations to meet the demands of donors instantaneously, and the reality that most charitable missions are not prepared to go to scale (Piper, 2019).

Once the carefully planned cause marketing partnership between Kentucky Fried Chicken and the Susan G. Komen Foundation infiltrated social networks, both brands suffered from the implied racial undertones and "pink-washing" of the [pink] "Buckets for a Cure" campaign, designed to target minority, female customers who frequent Kentucky Fried Chicken (CNN, 2010). Within a few weeks, the cause marketing campaign was canceled due to public backlash.

More recently, nonprofit organizations like Planned Parenthood, the ACLU, RAICES, and others have experienced extraordinary increases in donations since the 2016 election (Rinkunas, 2016). In January 2017 and in reaction to early official actions by newly inaugurated President Trump, the unprecedented response to the ACLU's "See You in Court" campaign (premeditated) resulted in several high-profile challenge gifts, and the ACLU website crashed as it struggled to cope with the internet traffic it received as people gave $24 million in one weekend (Blommel, 2017).

During our exploration of this recent phenomenon of rage giving, we explored some determinants of participation in rage giving: attitude toward giving online, social media intensity, and social influence. More positive attitudes toward donating online, more frequent use of social media platforms, and broader social networks (friends and followers) can influence decisions to act publicly in a selfless manner, as being associated with doing good increases reputation and feelings of altruism. However, first people have to become aware of the need, as a precursor to philanthropic action. In most rage giving, while the donations have been unsolicited, the demand has been made real and apparent through current events and social media activity.

Trust and commitment to a nonprofit will raise the intention to donate (Sargeant, Ford, & West, 2006). However, it is still unclear how social media use influences the pressure to donate (Lacetera, Macis, & Mele, 2014). Taylor et al. (2018) found that relationship satisfaction and identity salience moderated traditional determinants of charitable giving such as perceived trust, perceived organizational performance, demonstrable, familial and emotional utilities, parental socialization, youth experience, and satisfaction with the solicitation process. Taylor and Noble (2015) found that social media intensity, perceived trust in the nonprofit, emotional uplift, social media influence, and social pressure significantly predicted donors' charitable giving and participation in the ALS Association's Ice Bucket Challenge, while demonstrable utility, perceived commitment to the cause, and identity salience were not positively related to charitable giving. Viral donors did not have to have a personal connection or observe a tangible benefit from an organization to prompt viral giving. These previous research findings on viral giving suggest that attitudes and behaviors related to social media use are essential.

Given the nature of building social capital in one's community, online presence and online giving may be enough of a connection to build social capital. Yao (2015) describes social capital as "a combination of a number of connections and societal involvements, reciprocity of those relationships, political participation, and attitudes and perceptions of the local community" (p. 8). Membership in groups and networks, trust and solidarity, collective action and cooperation, information and communication, social cohesion and inclusion, and empowerment and political action are all dimensions of social capital (Grootaert et al., 2004). Participation in rage giving can be understood in a number of these dimensions, as illustrated by questions in the survey presented and described in Sections 1 and 2 of this Element.

In that survey, questions included the conceptual elements of attitudes toward donating online (Treiblmaier & Pollach, 2006) and social media intensity and influence (Ellison, Steinfeld, & Lampe, 2007). Attitudes toward giving online and social media intensity were measured using a seven-point scale of 1 = strongly disagree to 7 = strongly agree. Participants were asked to indicate their level of agreement on perceptions of online donating and social media use. Social media influence was measured by the number of hours spent online per week and the number of online friends.

Summary statistics in the random, nationwide sample ($N = 520$) are presented in Table 3. As expected in this study of rage giving and supported by the rapid increases in online giving, respondents had a more positive attitude toward donating online. Participants also reported higher levels of social media intensity, which indicates that more time spent on social media leads to more exposure to collective action and opportunities to give. Social media influence, or the self-reported size of respondents' networks, showed more variation in the sample, with a standard deviation of 3.9054.

Table 3 Social media and online giving

	Range	M	SD
Positive Attitude toward Donating Online	1–7	5.65	1.2852
Negative Attitude toward Donating Online	1–7	3.05	1.5940
Social Media Intensity	1–7	4.43	1.7216
Social Media Influence	2–15	8.16	3.9054

3.5 Summary

The confluence of early adopters of technology, its rapid diffusion, and the positive attitudes toward online giving allows nonprofit organizations to deepen relationships with supporters and develop a competitive advantage. According to the US Department of Commerce, as of February 2019, online shopping has grown in market share to 11.83 percent, surpassing the brick-and-mortar market share for the first time (2019). Online giving in the nonprofit sector has experienced a meteoric rise over the past few years, surpassing the percentage of market share in the retail market and following the overall migration of individual giving to online and other technologies. Positive attitudes toward online giving are driven by other purchase habits and perceived trust in online financial transactions.

As discussed in this section, the growth in the use of social media for personal and professional purposes has contributed to this overall migration in individual giving through online technologies. In the case of rage giving, the intensity of social media use contributes to increased exposure to online giving opportunities, civic engagement, and collective action. The public and nonprofit sectors have engaged the public in online community dialogues, town halls, and other civic engagement and policy advocacy activities through digital technology. The definition of community has expanded from the physical one in which people live, work, and play to a community definition that includes interactions and participation through social media, websites, and smartphones. As such, this has broad implications for marketing, communications, and fundraising strategy for nonprofit organizations. The knowledge, skills, and abilities that organizations need to gain this advantage, and to sustain it, have changed. Its proliferation has also increased possibilities for enhanced advocacy strategies, building stakeholder networks, and influencing public policies (Saxton, Guo, & Brown, 2007; Deschamps & McNutt, 2014; Guo & Saxton, 2014).

4 Intersecting Identities of Rage Givers

Central to understanding any phenomena is the consideration of the context in which it occurred; in this case, the intersecting identities of the individuals who participated in rage giving and what we can learn from their collective voices. Intersectionality originates in critical race theory and Black feminist theory. It describes how race, class, gender, and other individual characteristics "intersect" with one another and overlap, uncovering how these intersections present. These intersections and overlapping identities often lead to deep, structural, and systemic discrimination (Crenshaw, 1989). While the focus of this research on rage giving does not reflect a primary focus of intersectionality, there is an interesting sociodemographic pattern in the results that warrant further examination. We present some recent debates in intersectionality and emerging research in intersectional awareness as a theoretical framework for understanding the intersecting identities of rage givers. Following this discussion, we review the sociodemographic trends in charitable giving broadly in the USA and then compare those trends with the results represented in this investigation of rage giving. Additionally, we discuss these intersections in light of the behavioral response style.

4.1 Intersectionality and Intersectional Awareness

Intersectionality is situated in a long history of Black feminist writing and activism (Collins, 2011; Gines, 2014). Crenshaw's pivotal works describe the multidimensional experiences of Black women and the structural and systemic discrimination that resulted from their intersecting identities of being both Black and female, which are not mutually exclusive (1989). Crenshaw's essay focused on three legal cases that confronted issues of racial discrimination and gender discrimination: *DeGraffenreid* v. *General Motors*, *Moore* v. *Hughes Helicopter, Inc.*, and *Payne* v. *Travenol*. In each case, Crenshaw argued that the court's narrow interpretation of discrimination law seemed to overlook those Black women were both Black and female and were subject to discrimination with each of these identities and more often subject to more discrimination because of the overlapping identities. Several decades later, Crenshaw's theory of intersectionality, in which people experience discrimination differently based on their intersecting identities, became more mainstream and was a central focus of the 2017 Women's March in the United States. Critics of intersectionality argue that the multidimensional experiences of race and gender, among others, are clear; however, they are more concerned with whose responsibility it is to right those systemic and structural differences and at what cost.

At its core, intersectionality represents the observance and analysis of power imbalances. The framing of intersectionality has broadened since Crenshaw's (1989) original analysis, including analyzing power imbalances that comprise sexism, racism, class oppression, heterosexism, and other forms of oppression. As intersectionality has broadened and grown in acceptance, its application, and usefulness as a means for understanding the complexities of social inequality has become more prominent. More recent research suggests that *intersectional political consciousness*, or "a set of political beliefs and action orientations rooted in recognition of the need to account for multiple grounds of identity," can predict participation in collective action (Greenwood, 2008, p. 38). However, Greenwood's study examined group consciousness and did not account for individual differences in cognitive awareness of social inequalities, defined as *intersectional awareness*.

Curtin, Stewart, and Cole (2015) find that intersectional awareness can predict activism, the rejection of prejudicial attitudes and social inequalities, and collective action. Within this definition of intersectional awareness, individuals do not have to share an identity with a marginalized group to take action to right the imbalance or empathize with the experiences of the group. Other related research views this group as "engaged observers," those who express moral and financial support of social movements. Intersecting identities may facilitate motivation for building coalitions across group boundaries and empower social movements in pursuit of shared interests or in response to shared grievances (Crenshaw, 1991; Cole, 2008; Uluğ & Cohrs, 2017). More recent research about participation in the 2017 Women's March indicates that White women's motivations to protest for racial justice are related to the close relationships they have with members of marginalized groups (Tropp & Uluğ, 2019). We turn to the group and individual sociodemographic differences in charitable giving in the United States with the individual differences with social inequalities in mind or intersectional awareness.

4.2 Sociodemographics of Charitable Giving in the USA

According to Giving USA (2019), giving by individuals in the USA totaled an estimated \$292.09 billion, declining 1.1% in 2018 over 2017 (a decrease of 3.4%, adjusted for inflation). Changes in public policy for charitable giving and reporting amidst a complex philanthropic environment likely explain this small decrease to 68% of all charitable giving in 2018. Growth in charitable giving in the charitable sectors was mixed: giving to international affairs (+9.6%), environmental and animals increased (+3.6%), human services (−0.3%), health (+0.1%), and arts, culture, and humanities organizations (+0.3%) stayed relatively flat, while giving to public-society benefit (–3.7%), education (–1.5%), and religious organizations (–1.5%) decreased. The changes in charitable giving in the USA in 2018 reflect some changes that are contextually specific to the philanthropic environment in 2018. Still, the changes also reflect more long-term trends in giving as a whole. For example, giving to international affairs has experienced significant growth over several years, due in part to increasing globalization. In contrast, giving to religious organizations has decreased annually, as the religiously unaffiliated (atheist, agnostic, or "nothing in particular") in the USA has increased to 26% of the US population (Pew Research Center, 2015).

When looking at income, individuals with a higher income give the most in terms of dollar amounts. Still, lower-income individuals give an equal amount when viewing the available income given to charities. That is, when measuring charitable donations "as a fraction of the donor's income, giving is most robust at the top and bottom of the earnings spectrum" (The Philanthropy Roundtable, 2015). Those at the top 1 percent of income in the United States provide one-third of all charitable donations (Center on Philanthropy at Indiana University, 2010). Also, current household incomes have a significant impact on donations, whereas previous household incomes do not (Yao, 2015).

When considering age, individuals tend to give more to charities in their retirement years, with 77% of households with those ages 61–75 donating, compared to 60% of households with 26–45-year olds (The Philanthropy Roundtable, 2015). By and large, as people age, they become more involved in their communities as their desires to give increase (Andreoni, Brown, & Rischall, 2003; Lee & Chang, 2007).

With regard to ethnicity, White donors are the largest group of individuals giving to charitable organizations, with 73% of donors today being non-Hispanic Whites. African Americans and Hispanics are underrepresented compared to their overall population size, as they make up 9% and 11% of the total donor pool. Asians make up 5% of the donor pool (Blackbaud Institute, 2015). However, when looking at charitable giving as a share of median family wealth, households with people of color are giving at a higher percentage than White households (Ashley & James, 2018). This higher rate of giving may be attributed to cultures of giving in Black communities, which emphasize family traditions of giving, fulfillment from giving, long-term commitments to giving, and organized networks of organizations that facilitate charitable giving (Ashley & James, 2018). Ethnicity, however, is not found to have a significant impact on the amount given to charitable organizations, but it does impact where individuals give (IUPUI Women's Philanthropy Institute, 2019).

In one study reviewing philanthropy across ethnicity and gender, it was found that single women donate more than single men across all racial and ethnic groups, and married couples often give the most to charitable organizations (IUPUI Women's Philanthropy Institute, 2019). However, this finding is somewhat contradicted by another study that finds that married couples are more likely to donate than singles. Still, single females are not more likely to donate than single males (Yao, 2015).

In some studies, highly educated individuals have been found to donate more and to be more altruistic (Yen, 2002; Andreoni, Brown, & Rischall, 2003). This connection tends to result from a general awareness of societal issues and a feeling of being more fortunate than others (Yao, 2015).

Political affiliation does not appear to have a significant relationship with donating, although parties are thought to be aligned with specific types of donating. Democrats tend to support welfare programs, and Republicans' give money through their taxes (Brooks, 2006).

While not significant, employment is also a factor in giving as those who are employed are more likely willing to donate, especially those who have a steady income. Those who are retired or unemployed tend to give less, but instead give time by volunteering (Yao, 2015). The opportunity costs associated with charitable giving prevail. With the previous literature in mind, we now turn to explore the sociodemographics of individuals participating in rage giving.

4.3 Sociodemographics in Rage Giving

One of the fundamental rules of fundraising is the "three Cs:" capacity to give, commitment to giving, and connection to the cause. The capacity to give alone is not enough to generate donations; donors must also demonstrate a commitment and connection to the mission. In the rage giving study and data presented throughout this Elements, two-thirds of the respondents (n = 393) report an annual household income of $99,999 or below with the most respondents coming from annual household incomes of less than $50,000 ($n$ = 162). These findings support and further emphasize that charitable giving, including giving motivated by rage, is more robust at lower incomes than higher incomes. Almost half of the respondents (48%, n = 250) are engaged in full-time employment, with the next largest group being retired individuals (27%, n = 118). Part-time workers made up 14% of the respondents (n = 73), with the remaining categories as 5% or less of respondents. These results support findings more broadly in charitable giving research in that those working with a steady income are most likely to give. However, as presented above, those with a lower annual household income were most likely to make a rage gift.

The age of respondents was also distributed across categories as individuals between the ages of: 18–29 (24%, n = 125), 30–39 (19%, n = 101), 40–49 (13.4%, n = 70), 50–59 (12.9%, n = 67), 60–69 (20.4%, n = 106), 70–79 (9%, n = 47), and 80 or older (0.8%, n = 4). Middle-aged individuals comprised a quarter of the respondents, with 26.3% of individuals being between the ages of 40 and 59. These results contrast with giving behaviors more broadly as the most salient age group were the youngest (18–29) and the middle-aged (40–59). Of particular interest is the prominence of Generation X and Millennials in the survey results.

Considering the ethnic identity of respondents, the sample is skewed, with 80% of respondents reporting White (n = 417). The next largest category is Black or African American at 6% (n = 32), closely followed by Hispanic/ Latino/Spanish origin (n = 31) and Asian (n = 23). The remaining categories of ethnicity are in the single digits. This distribution mirrors the trends in charitable giving more broadly. However, when coupled with the generational and income patterns, it presents another point of interest.

Gender is more evenly distributed across the sample with 58% (n = 300) of respondents reporting female and 41% (n = 215) reporting male. Five respondents reported either trans female, genderqueer, or gender nonconforming. These results do not support the existing literature that women give more than men, broadly. In the context of rage giving, the results indicate that giving motivated by anger is shared across gender identities.

Education shows variation across categories, with 51 percent (n = 265) of respondents having an undergraduate degree or graduate degree. The two categories with the most responses are baccalaureate degree (n = 150) and some college but not a degree (n = 111). This is followed by respondents with graduate degrees (n = 71), high school graduates (n = 63), and associate degrees (n = 57). The remaining categories had twenty-one respondents or less. In contrast to the existing giving literature, these results indicate that those with less education are more likely to participate in rage giving.

Political party affiliation is made up of 44% (n = 229) Democrats, 25% (n = 128) Republicans, and 28% (n = 146) Independents. These results are in contrast to charitable giving research, which finds that political affiliation does not influence giving behaviors. However, the timing of the distribution of this survey in the first quarter after the presidential election in the USA is potentially reflected in the political affiliation of the sample.

The limitations of this study should be reiterated. As noted prior, the sample is overly skewed White (80%), the majority of respondents identify as Democrats (44%), and nearly half of the respondents have an annual household income of $99,000 or less. The categorical representation in the sample may have influenced the results, and future studies in this area warrant more attention to sampling bias. Regardless, the data presented here do present relevant, interesting, and insightful results for us to consider.

We also evaluated the relationship between age and gender, education, ethnicity, income, employment, and political affiliation through cross-tabulation, as illustrated in Tables 4–6. The data were analyzed using the chi-square goodness-of-fit test. There was no significant relationship between age and gender, age and income, or age and political affiliation. Not surprisingly, there was a significant relationship between age and education, $X 2(70) =$ 122.176, $p \geq 0.05$, meaning that as people age, they gain a more formal education. However, it is important to keep in mind education across the sample of rage givers, and in contrast to giving research, those with less education are more likely to make a rage gift. Age and ethnicity were also related, $X 2(70) =$ 137.565, $p \geq 0.05$. Across all age groups, respondents were most likely to report

Table 4 Chi-square tests age and education

	Value	df	Asymptomatic Significance (Two-Sided)
Pearson Chi-Square	122.176[a]	80	0.002
Likelihood Ratio	131.954	80	0.000
Linear-by-Linear Association	32.095	1	0.000
No. of Valid Cases	520		

[a] 60 cells (60.6 percent) have an expected count of less than 5. The minimum expected count is 0.07.

Table 5 Chi-square tests age and ethnicity

	Value	df	Asymptomatic Significance (Two-Sided)
Pearson Chi-Square	137.565[a]	70	0.000
Likelihood Ratio	110.555	70	0.001
Linear-by-Linear Association	10.395	1	0.001
No. of Valid Cases	520		

[a] 76 cells (86.4 percent) have an expected count of less than 5. The minimum expected count is 0.01.

Table 6 Chi-square tests age and employment

	Value	df	Asymptomatic Significance (two-sided)
Pearson Chi-Square	392.387[a]	60	0
Likelihood Ratio	401.665	60	0
Linear-by-Linear Association	29.609	1	0
No. of Valid Cases	520		

[a] 48 cells (62.3 percent) have an expected count of less than 5. The minimum expected count is 0.07.

their ethnicity as White. Age and employment were related, $X2(60) = 392.387$, $p \geq 0.05$.

Within rage givers, there are interesting intersections of identity, particularly as it relates to age and ethnicity. Looking at the results through the lens of generational identity provides the opportunity to view rage givers both by their place in the life cycle – a young adult, a middle-aged parent, or a retiree – and by their membership in a cohort of individuals who were born at a similar time. Anyone born between 1981 and 1996 (ages 25–40 in 2022) is considered a Millennial, and anyone born from 1997 onward is part of a new generation, Generation Z (Pew Research Center, 2015). Anyone born between 1965 and 1980 (ages 41–56 in 2022) is considered a member of Generation X. Each generation is characterized by the dynamic social, political, scientific, economic, and technological contexts that shape their lived experiences and perspectives. Rage givers are more likely to be members of the Millennial or Generation X generations.

Generation X are the children of Baby Boomers (1946–1964) and, in 2022, are aged 41–56 years. Sociologically, Generation X was shaped by the frequency with which their parents divorced, the rapid increase of women joining the workforce outside the home, and without access to childcare, thus being dubbed the "latchkey" generation. Generation X has grown to be known for their entrepreneurial mindset, the diffusion of technology in everyday life, and distinctly influenced by the political and economic markers of their lifetimes (the fall of the Berlin Wall and communism, Gulf War I, 9/11 terrorist attacks, the 1980s Recession, and the Great Recession). Finally, the Corporation for National and Community Service reports in 2017 that Generation X has the highest volunteering rate compared with other generations, 36.4 percent per year.

Millennials are just old enough to have been shaped by the events of the 9/11 terrorist attacks in the USA and have grown up under the shadow of the wars in Iraq and Afghanistan. Millennials are considered the most racially and ethnically diverse adults in history. Reaching adulthood during an economic recession, these circumstances have shaped their life choices, future earnings, and entrance to adulthood. Most important to rage giving, Millennials are digital natives and express great ease with the adoption of digital technology and social media. Likewise, Millennials vote at a higher rate as compared with Generation X at the same age (Galston, 2017). In a study of alumni giving in independent colleges, Harvard (2019) finds that among Millennials, the higher the perception that other alumni give, the stronger was their intention to donate. According to Gorczyca and Hartman (2017), "Millennials prefer to donate to a cause, not an organization" and believe that sharing their time and knowledge and spreading the word about a cause are more important than their making a monetary gift (p. 425). Harnett and Matan (2014) found that peer solicitations and peer support for and involvement with a charity/cause increase Generation Y's motivation to donate time and money (Gorczyca & Hartman, 2017; Kupperschmidt, 2000).

Currently, the majority of philanthropy is given by members of the Silent Generation (born before 1944) and Baby Boomers (born between 1945 and 1964). However, 51 percent of political and economic leadership positions globally are held by members of Generation X (Deloitte, 2019) who, by 2030, are expected to hold 31 percent of America's wealth. WealthEngine (2019) reports an expected wealth transfer of $68 trillion to Millennials over the next twenty-five years. Goldseker and Moody (2017) report that Generation X and Millennials are focused on the impact of giving and "seeing that my contribution makes a real difference, and the organization has real impact." They want to move the needle on the causes of which they care most.

The causes they care about are not necessarily the causes of their parents or even their friends. Notoriously independent and coming of age before the immediacy and influence of social media, Generation X is sandwiched between digital natives (Baby Boomers) and digital natives (Millennials). Both Generation X and Millennials possess liberal views on key policy issues: the role of government, the environment, the acceptance of homosexuality, race, immigration, and diplomacy (Dimock, 2019). It is essential to consider how these generations perceive social inequality, participate in collective action, and reflect their attitudes toward political participation because it could predict future charitable giving.

Cole and Stewart (1996) find that social responsibility among Black and White women who attended college in the 1960s is associated with midlife political participation. They were influenced by the social movements of that era, including women who did not actively participate in social activism. Called "engaged observers" were individuals who were "attentive to movement writings and activities" and expressed moral and financial support for the social movements. In the case of rage giving, the confluence of digital technology, social media, online giving, and dissatisfaction with the political climate enabled engaged observers to take action through charitable giving. Curtin, Stewart, and Cole (2015) investigated the antecedents and implications of intersectional awareness, finding that intersectional awareness was related to basic personality traits, beliefs about the social status quo, prosocial attitudes toward out-groups, and the intention to be politically active. More intersections of identity in rage giving are explored in variations among rage givers in behavioral anger response style.

4.4 Rage Giving and Anger Response Style

It is not evident in the research on the emotional benefits of charitable giving how negative emotions might influence giving behavior. Consequently, we consider the role of anger and rage, as identified in the Geneva Emotion Wheel as active and intense negative feelings (Bänziger, Tran, & Scherer, 2005) in charitable giving. Research on different forms of anger behavior provides a foundation that can be applied to rage giving since understanding how one behaves when angry has been researched extensively (Markus & Kitayama, 1991; Bushman, 2002; Kuppens et al., 2004; von Salisch & Vogelgesang, 2005; Miers et al., 2007). Linden et al. (2003) use Arnold's (1960) definition of anger as a short-term emotion triggered by specific events, and the meaning of the individual identifies with those events. Anger responses explained as anger-in and anger-out have been commonly researched. Venting anger has been found to suppress the emotions associated with anger, but people must direct this emotion toward the one who angered them. They need to believe that there will not be retaliation.

In 1992, Buss and Perry developed *The Aggression Questionnaire* identifying four dimensions: physical aggression, verbal aggression, anger, and hostility. They were one of the first to overlay these anger variables with what they called other personality traits, of which assertiveness is included. In their work, assertiveness correlated strongly with anger. Assertive behavior was later defined as "confronting the provoking person but without overt verbal or physical aggression" (O'Connor, Archer, & Wu, 2001). It became clear that anger-in and anger-out were not the only ways to respond when angry. O'Conner et al. found aggression and assertiveness to be disconnected and determined that these were alternative responses (2001). However, it could be argued that assertiveness is a form of anger-in. One is more likely to express anger-in when the person they are angry at is disliked (Kuppens et al., 2004).

Linden et al. (2003) further refined the variations in anger response style in the Behavioral Anger Response Questionnaire (BARQ). The six anger response styles are direct anger-out, assertion, social support-seeking, diffusion, avoidance, and rumination. Direct anger-out and avoidance reflect the two extremes of anger coping styles: aggression and passivity or suppression. Three moderate or adaptive anger coping styles are assertion, diffusion, and social support-seeking. Assertion refers to the ability to express one's anger or solve the angering event constructively. Diffusion entails deflecting the anger to another stimulus or activity. Social support-seeking refers to seeking support from a friend or relative. The sixth anger coping style is rumination, which describes the tendency to cope with one's anger to be repeatedly deliberating over its cause. In rage giving, we find that direct anger-out, diffusion, and rumination to be the most significant anger response styles in rage givers.

The following are the results from the chi-square and Cramér's V statistical analyses. Only statistically significant relationships between categories of demographics and behavioral responses to anger are shown and explained. Effect sizes are also reported to illustrate the strength of the relationship between variables.

Those rage givers who reported an anger response style of *direct anger-out*, age, and ethnicity were statistically significant, indicating a relationship between direct anger-out and age, with a small to moderate effect size, 0.182. The relationship between direct anger-out and ethnicity has a moderate effect, 0.196. Ethnicity and age in rage giving co-vary and are not independent of one another. White respondents and 18–49-year olds reported direct anger-out as "not true," leaning to "sometimes true." Those 50 years old or older and American Indian/Alaskan Native/Asian/other reported direct anger-out as "sometimes true." Those respondents of Hispanic/Latino/Spanish origin reported "sometimes true," leaning to "not true." Those respondents of Black/African American origin reported direct anger-out as "not true."

Of those rage givers who reported an anger response style of *diffusion*, age, and employment were statistically significant, with a small to moderate effect size of 0.182 and diffusion and employment with a small effect size of 0.150. Age and employment in those who reported an anger response style of diffusion are not independent of one another. Currently, unemployed or full-time students, aged 18–24, reported an anger response style of "sometimes true" to "often true." Those rage givers working full time, part time, and 25–54 years old reported diffusion as an anger response style of "sometimes true." Those aged

55 years and older, retired, or stay-at-home parents reported an anger response style of diffusion as "sometimes true," leaning to "not true."

Of those rage givers who reported *social support-seeking*, household income, and employment are statistically significant, indicating that there is a relationship between social support-seeking and household income, the effect size is small to moderate, 0.156. Employment and social support-seeking are also significant; the effect size is small to moderate, 0.158. Household income and employment are not independent of each other. Of those rage givers earning less than $50,000–$99,000 per year, $200,000–$249,000, and $250,000 per year or more, working full time, part time, unemployed, or full-time stay-at-home parents reported social support-seeking as "sometimes true." Those earning $100,000–$149,000, $150,000–$199,000, and retired reported social support seeking as "sometimes true," leaning to "not true." Full-time students reported "sometimes true," leaning to "often true."

Of those rage givers who reported *rumination* as an anger response style, there is a statistically significant relationship between rumination and political affiliation; the effect size is small to moderate, 0.184. All political party affiliations reported rumination as "sometimes true" leaning to "often true."

There were no significant relationships between *assertion* or *avoidance* and any of the demographic variables. In contrast to Linden et al. (2003), in which women reported the use of a broader range of anger coping styles, especially social support seeking and anger diffusion than men, gender was found to be not significant in rage givers. Educational attainment level and anger response style were also found not to be significant.

In summary, we find that direct anger-out, diffusion, and rumination to be the most significant anger response styles in rage givers. Direct anger-out is related to age and ethnicity, in particular, White Millennials and Generation X. Diffusion is related to age and employment. Rumination is related to political affiliation, across party lines.

4.5 Summary

Overall, the intersections of identity reflected in rage giving also mirror the growing diversity in the United States and the confluence of digital technology, social media, online giving, and collective action. People view charitable giving as a viable means of political protest and philanthropy as a means of social change. Empathetic anger results in action and is linked to political mobilization. We posit that rage givers exhibit higher levels of empathetic anger and intersectional awareness and are thus able to see the social injustice experienced by marginalized groups and desire to funnel that anger into positive action. Politics may trigger emotions that have short-term motivational impacts, as is the case in rage giving. We can also assume that an individual's desire to donate out of anger is prosocial behavior, which is influenced by individual experiences, ideologies, and communities. Charitable giving, even in the form of small gifts, and gifts made out of anger can build social capital by building a community and network of rage givers who donated in response to triggering events and the political climate.

Rage giving is a thought-out behavior in response to an emotion, and the response itself is social or cultural. Actions taken to donate in response to the political climate, founded in emotions of anger or rage, are driven from the climate one observes or the social movements one wants to be a part of. It is this collective action that may provide an individual the satisfaction of changing an undesirable situation or simply giving that individual a form to express their displeasure.

5 The Future of Philanthropy and Rage Giving as a Social Movement

In the years during and after the 2016 presidential election, giving out of an emotional response to anger received a salient and catchy label, that of rage giving (Rage Donate, 2017; Segedin, 2018). Simply put, rage giving is a phenomenon that connects negative emotions to giving (McHugh, 2018). Since the election, donating as a response to the political climate has appeared to be a new and exciting paradigmatic shift in philanthropy and giving, and it is gaining traction. Rage giving illustrates that behavior and sentiment are both critical factors in motivating an individual to donate, often driven by an individual's values (Lee, 2018).

As politicians, political activists, and citizens become more divided and thus more expressive, rage giving is making its mark as a way to communicate the displeasure of the people. Displeasure in the construct of "satisfaction with life in America" continues to be debated in the news media, on social media, in academic circles, and during dinner-table conversations. Many Americans feel an innate desire to create change in the social systems of our communities and our country, and this desire has resulted in more civic engagement activities and behavioral responses to social and political injustices impacting the everyday citizen (Doolittle & Faul, 2013). Individual satisfaction with the state of America appears to directly influence one's behavior, and civic engagement has been linked to a person's overall well-being (Albanesi, Cicognani, & Zani, 2007). In one study, the community feeling created through social media use positively correlated with social capital and life satisfaction

(Valenzuela, Park, & Kee, 2009). In another study, expressing anger was associated with increased satisfaction with life in America (Mayer, 2020). On the contrary, holding in anger has been found to create less life satisfaction and increased depression, anxiety, and other health disorders (Watkins, 2004; Mayer, 2020). Rage giving can be a healthy response to negative emotions related to social and political injustice.

In addition, levels of optimism toward life in America tend to rise and fall depending on one's political affiliation (Graham & Pinto, 2017; Swift, 2016), as is evident in the political discussions and debates over the Trump Administration's response to the COVID-19 epidemic of 2020. According to the Pew Research Center, 83% of Republican-leaning citizens believe the Trump Administration's response to the pandemic was excellent, and only 18% of Democratic-leaning citizens agreed with this sentiment (Pew Research Center, 2020). As a counter to critics of the Trump Administration's handling of COVID-19, Trump and his key Republican supporters accused the World Health Organization (WHO) of being biased in favor of China, not accurately tracking the spread of the virus, and releasing false information about the virus (Beaumont & Burke, 2020; Green & Tyson, 2020). On April 14, 2020, the Trump Administration froze US funding to the WHO for sixty to ninety days, pending an investigation, a move that sent public health officials reeling (Baker & Hincks, 2020). Critics of the decision viewed it as an "appalling betrayal of global solidarity" and a "crime against humanity" (Corbet, 2020). Days later, the international advocacy group Global Citizen hosted an already planned eight-hour virtual event called "One World: Together at Home" that brought together musicians and performers from around the world to raise money for frontline healthcare workers and the WHO. This event raised $127.9 million in pledged donations toward organizations responding to COVID-19 and $55.1 million for the WHO's Solidarity Response Fund (Lee, 2020). People wanted their voices heard by making donations in support of both the healthcare workers and the WHO and as a backlash to the Trump Administration's decision to freeze the WHO's funding.

With rage giving's relevance to most political climates, it is evident that individual donors attempt to build social capital and participate in civic engagement by donating to nonprofit organizations. Nonprofit organizations are an essential component of building social capital, creating systemic change, aiding the underprivileged and underserved, and bringing citizens together with a shared goal. As Flanagan (2003) notes, "people are more likely to act on behalf of the group when they identify with the group" (p. 257).

The next section explores strategies and considerations of rage giving as a future marketing and philanthropic tool of nonprofit organizations. Rage giving is discussed as a positive strategy for nonprofit organizations, including tips for practitioners interested in this approach. This is followed by a discussion of the negative consequences and considerations of rage giving as a fundraising strategy. Since rage giving is a newly recognized form of giving by nonprofit organizations, both the pragmatic and unexpected consequences of integrating this form of giving into a nonprofit organization's strategic plan must be explored.

5.1 The Pros of Rage Giving as a Fundraising Tool

Rage giving is a paradigmatic shift in philanthropy and giving, and the strategy has become more apparent as the political divide increases in the United States. This form of giving is a common method for individuals to express emotions of anger to promote liberty and equality (Venkatesh, 2002). With its growing popularity, rage giving must be taken seriously in that it provides a new lens for nonprofit organizations' marketing and fundraising strategies. Nonprofit organizations' strategic planning sessions can develop marketing and communications plans that harness the anger of citizens in the community and customers of the nonprofit, encouraging them to participate in civic engagement activities such as rage giving (see Table 7).

When targeting the positive impacts and advantages of rage giving on an individual, nonprofit organizations wishing to mobilize individuals acting on emotion can tout that "political goals are achieved by collective action" (Flanagan, 2003, p. 257). And "civically engaged individuals may decide to come together in response to some issue, event, or need" (Hyman, 2002, p. 198). This results in shared resources and knowledge that can contribute to social and political movements.

Nonprofit organizations can rely on individuals' feelings of emotional uplift when donors participate in rage giving. Donors making a rage gift genuinely

Table 7 Individual benefits of rage giving

Rage giving:
- provides an opportunity to participate in civic engagement,
- creates a venue for collective action,
- offers a space to share resources and knowledge that may contribute toward a social or political movement/cause,
- results in a feeling of emotional uplift,
- makes a difference by expressing a voice and opinion,
- produces something action-oriented,
- represents a healthy way to respond to negative emotions,
- is convenient and easy to do online, and
- provides a way to contribute instead of volunteering time.

believe they are making a difference in their community. By rage donating, angry individuals can feel like they are doing something productive and action-oriented, and that giving is a normal reaction to negative emotion. They may not wish to volunteer their time or have the capacity to volunteer, but they are more than happy to get online and donate to a cause as an emotional response to a social or political issue. Also, giving online is convenient and straightforward to do – it is at an individual's fingertips (Ferry, 2017).

As a strategic planning initiative, nonprofit organizations need to prepare for moments when rage giving and virtual donating might be a primary tactic that contributes to the organization's fundraising goals, one that is spawned by a perceived social or political injustice. Nonprofit organizations can strategize to create an alignment between their mission and giving and civic engagement opportunities for individuals in the community (see Table 8). To prepare, nonprofit organizations need to train staff and board members on key messages they can use to talk with donors and other stakeholders about the emotional

Table 8 Rage giving marketing and fundraising strategies

Consider these actions when developing strategic plans:

- Target younger generations since they are more inclined to participate in rage giving than older generations
- Control the narrative on policy and community issues that impact the non-profit organization's stakeholders:
  - Train staff, board members, and volunteers to talk with donors about emotional impacts of issues affecting the nonprofit's mission
  - Update the website content to clarify the organization's position on a social or policy issue
  - Put out press releases stating the position of the nonprofit
  - Utilize live, in-the-moment storytelling on social media
- Create long-term planning around rage donating – strategize how to appeal to, and mobilize, angry donors:
  - Develop marketing and communications plans to drive engagement
  - Write a nonprofit advocacy plan that supports civic engagement
- Embrace strategic thinking about public policy and current events and build capacity:
  - Anticipate future social and political events that might lead to rage giving
  - Prepare for moments when rage giving and virtual donating might be a primary tactic of donor giving
  - Have an emergency donation page ready in anticipation of an episodic moment of giving
  - Conversely, think about the communications strategy for post-rage giving and develop a donor retention plan

issues impacting the nonprofit organization's mission, harnessing any feelings of anger donors may be feeling toward a particular social or political injustice. In some cases, these issues may not relate to the political climate and may refer to an environmental or social concern. Nonprofit organizations should also find a way to utilize volunteers to help disseminate the narrative of the nonprofit organization to the community in a friendly and unobtrusive way.

In addition, nonprofit organizations should control the narrative on policy and community issues that impact their stakeholders so that long-term planning for rage donations can be achieved. This includes updating the nonprofit organization's website to reflect the organization's stance on specific social or policy issues, making sure not to lose sight of its mission. The website should offer toolkits for action for community members and donors that will inform these individuals of different ways to participate in civic engagement, including rage donating. Nonprofit organizations should also consider having an emergency donation page ready for when it might be needed since rage giving and the events it transpires from are episodic (Waasdorp, 2018). Furthermore, nonprofit organizations should utilize social media as a way to disseminate a specific narrative through storytelling. Younger generations should be targeted since they are more likely to participate in rage giving than older generations (Lee, 2018).

Nonprofit organizations should embrace strategic thinking about public policy, current events, building capacity, and social capital, in addition to encouraging civic participation by adopting a nonprofit advocacy plan that supports civic engagement and action. By embracing this approach to strategic thinking, nonprofit organizations can find a way to solve the challenge of "link[ing] advocacy to strengthening the organization's message" (Bass et al., 2007, p. 517). In short, nonprofit organizations need to determine how to appeal to and motivate angry citizens who want an outlet to express their anger. Many events that spawn emotional outcries can be predicted if staff follow local, state, and national politics. Thus, marketing and communications plans can be drafted to drive engagement when anticipated events do happen.

Finally, nonprofit organizations need to determine the aftermath of a rage giving fundraising tool since the events that spawned the outrage and giving may be short-lived (Waasdorp, 2018). A donor retention plan is necessary, and nonprofit organizations should consider sending a quick, impactful, and overly powerful thank-you message immediately after the donation happens. Also, after the donation is made, consider communicating with the donors about the impact of their gift through a video or visual that illustrates the effect of the contribution on the mission. Also, keeping the donor updated with information that will make them feel good about their monetary gift will encourage the individual to give again. Learning about the motivations of donors enables nonprofit organizations to align their fundraising strategies with the passions of their support base.

There are many positive aspects of integrating rage giving as part of the nonprofit organization's strategic plan and fundraising approach. While this approach may be successful and may produce additional funding for the organization while raising awareness of the nonprofit organization's mission, some cautions and considerations must be taken into account. Next, we discuss the concerns raised against the use of rage giving as a fundraising tool.

5.2 The Cons of Rage Giving as a Fundraising Tool

Since there are varying perceptions and intentions of different approaches to philanthropy, it is essential to consider the negative impacts of rage giving as a fundraising tool for individuals and nonprofit organizations. While rage giving is thought to be an extension of activism, not everyone agrees (Hodges, 2018). Thus, while rage giving may present itself as a new, relevant, and attractive method for fundraising, it also has its critics. Given this trepidation, it is essential to address the reasons why rage giving may not be a productive philanthropic tool for a nonprofit organization (see Table 9).

The first note of caution for nonprofit organizations is that rage giving is episodic and tied to specific disasters and events (MacLaughlin, 2017). This reason alone creates difficulties with planning, budgeting, and the reliability of donors who give based on an emotional response to a social or political injustice that is happening during a given period. While many social and political injustices can be predicted, many cannot. For this reason, a nonprofit organization may be hesitant to adopt rage giving as a tactic in their fundraising strategy, especially when resources and capacity are constrained.

Table 9 Considerations of rage giving

Before engaging in a rage giving strategy, nonprofits should consider the following:
- It may crowd out other forms of civic engagement that would be better suited for voicing concerns.
- It may not be anger that drives the donations; it may be fear or simply contribution to the mission.
- The worry that "policy advocacy" may result in losing grant funding.
- "Rage" has a negative connotation.
- It is episodic, not consistent, and tied to specific episodes and events.
- An episodic event may not be perceived the same by everyone.
- An impression may be given that the nonprofit is capitalizing off of tragedy or negativity.

In addition, an event that elicits anger emotions in one individual may not evoke the same feelings in another, thus adding to the complexity of harnessing rage as a motivator for giving (Hodges, 2018). Rather than donating out of a feeling of rage or anger, it is possible that individuals donate to a nonprofit organization out of fear or simply want to contribute to the value of the mission. If this is the case, marketing, communications, and fundraising strategies built on motivating individuals to give out of rage or anger may be moot and ineffective.

Nonprofit organizations must also be mindful of the negative connotation of the word "rage" in their marketing, communications, and fundraising materials. Individual donors may be turned off from a nonprofit organization that gives the impression it is capitalizing on tragedy or negativity (Hodges, 2018). Besides building supporters, donors may wonder why the nonprofit organization is promoting negative messages, and the mission of the organization may be muted by the emotional emphasis of the episodic fundraising drive, usually driven by anger.

Furthermore, some nonprofit organizations may be hesitant to develop a rage giving fundraising strategy because those efforts may mimic activities similar to policy advocacy, and this may result in the nonprofit organization losing eligibility for grant funding (Leroux & Goerdel, 2009). Many grant funders prohibit policy advocacy or lobbying activities, and a nonprofit organization's fundraising strategy focusing on rage giving may be incorrectly viewed as advocacy, since rage giving is often a reaction to a political or policy issue and the nonprofit organization may be taking a stance on that issue. Since nonprofit organizations need to be careful in their approach to political, advocacy, and protest activities (Schmid, Bar, & Nirel, 2008), they should thoughtfully strategize any approach to rage giving as a fundraising tool to ensure it will not prevent a nonprofit organization from receiving future grant funding or jeopardizing its nonprofit status.

Finally, it is also possible that rage giving is crowding out other forms of civic engagement that might be better suited to voice concerns of citizens on social and political injustices (Mayer, 2020).

While rage giving expresses a voice through donating and dollars, other civic engagement tools such as marching or disseminating information through social media may be more powerful and may create a better sense of community. As such, nonprofit organizations should support their rage giving donors, but they may also want to encourage them to participate in another form of civic action.

While the list of negative aspects of rage giving as a fundraising tool is relatively short, it is not something to ignore. If a nonprofit organization adopts rage giving in its fundraising toolkit, the organization needs to be prepared to respond to board members' concerns and citizens' potential negative perceptions of the organization's approach. It is possible a rage giving strategy could hurt the organization's reputation, rather than help with fundraising.

5.3 Summary

There are obvious benefits for individuals to participate in rage giving. Most notably, giving provides individuals with a feeling of uplift and a sense of taking action. Since younger generations are more reliant than ever on social media and online platforms to receive their daily information and news, online giving will likely continue to grow. Millennials, in particular, demonstrate healthy prosocial behaviors (Paulin et al., 2014), and they are often characterized as "civically involved, socially conscious, [and] interested in helping others and solving the problems of the world" (Ertas, 2016, p. 518).

Given Millennials' reliance on, and skills navigating, the Internet and their propensity to be socially-minded, it is likely rage giving will continue to be an outlet for expressions of anger.

There is little doubt individual donors will continue to feel emotions of rage and anger in response to social and political injustices, and rage giving will continue as a reply to this anger. The question, then, is whether this new trend in giving will be recognized and adopted in the strategic plans of nonprofit organizations as a fundraising, marketing, or communications tool and whether nonprofit organizations will become dependent on this type of episodic giving, with some writing this line item into their budgets.

The pros and cons of adopting a rage giving fundraising strategy are definite, yet the decision to take this leap of faith is muddled. If the nonprofit organization is willing to commit staff and resources to track political, social, and policy issues, it may be possible to predict an event that will elicit rage and anger in donors. If that is the case, a rage giving strategy may make sense. Nonprofit organizations should be tracking political, social, and policy issues concerning their mission anyway. If a nonprofit organization cannot provide this level of attention to external events that may impact donors, it may not be sensible to consider rage giving as a fundraising, marketing, or communications strategy. However, if the nonprofit organization's mission is likely to be impacted by externalities, the nonprofit may want to put a contingency plan in place for the moment the episodic event arrives. During this time, the nonprofit can capitalize on angry donors.

The future of rage giving as a fundraising strategy for nonprofit organizations is unknown, and it is unpredictable whether organizations can rely on this type of funding. But, for now, rage giving makes both individuals and nonprofit organizations feel like they are part of a more significant social movement, and that may be enough to motivate rage givers to continue donating when they are feeling the need to take action for a cause.

References

Adena, M., & Hager, A. (2020). Does online fundraising increase charitable giving? A nation-wide field experiment on Facebook. WZB Discussion Paper No. SP II 2020–302. www.econstor.eu/handle/10419/215415

Adjei, D., Annor-Frempong, F., & Bosompem, M. (2016). Use of social networking websites among NGOs in the greater accra region of Ghana. *Public Relations Review*, *42*(5), 920–928.

Albanesi, C., Cicognani, E., & Zani, B. (2007). Sense of community, civic engagement and social well-being in Italian adolescents. *Journal of Community & Applied Social Psychology*, *17*(5), 387–406.

ALS Association. (n.d.). Dedicated to Finding a Cure for ALS. *ALS Association*. www.als.org/

Anderson, B. (2017). Tweeter-in-Chief: A content analysis of President Trump's tweeting habits. *Elon Journal of Undergraduate Research in Communications*, *8*(2), 36–47.

Andreoni, J., Brown, E., & Rischall, I. (2003). Charitable giving by married couples who decides and why does it matter? *Journal of Human Resources*, *38*(1), 111–133.

Andreoni, J., & Rao, J. (2011). The power of asking: How communication affects selfishness, empathy, and altruism. *Journal of Public Economics*, *95* (7–8), 513–520.

Arnold, M. B. (1960). *Emotion and personality*. Columbia University Press.

Ashley, S., & James, J. (2018, February 28). Despite the racial wealth gap, black philanthropy is strong. *The Urban Institute*. www.urban.org/urban-wire/despite-racial-wealth-gap-black-philanthropy-strong

Baker, A., & Hincks, J. (2020, April 17). What Trump's WHO funding freeze means for the most vulnerable countries. *Time*. https://time.com/5823297/trump-who-funding-freeze-africa-coronavirus/

Bänziger, T., Tran, V., & Scherer, K. R. (2005). The Emotion Wheel. A Tool for the Verbal Report of Emotional Reactions, *Poster Presented at the Conference of the International Society of Research on Emotion, Bari, Italy.*

Bass, G., Arons, D., Guinane, K., & Carter, M. (2007). *Seen but not heard: Strengthening nonprofit advocacy.* Washington, DC: The Aspen Institute.

Batson, C. (2012). A history of prosocial behavior research. In A. W. Kruglanski & W. Stroebe (Eds.), *Handbook of the history of social psychology* (pp. 243–264). Psychology Press, Hove, East Sussex, United Kingdom.

Beaumont, P., & Burke, J. (2020, April 8). Now is not the time to cut WHO funds, says official after Trump threat. *The Guardian.* www.theguardian.com/world/2020/apr/08/now-is-not-the-time-to-cut-who-funds-says-official-after-trump-threat

Bekkers, R., & Wiepking, P. (2007, October). Understanding philanthropy: A review of 50 years of theories and research. *Research Presented at the 35th Annual Conference of the Association for Research on Nonprofit and Voluntary Action, Chicago.*

Bellucci, G., Camilleri, J. A., Eickhoff, S. B., & Krueger, F. (2020). Neural signatures of prosocial behaviors. *Neuroscience & Biobehavioral Reviews, 118*(1), 186–195. http://doi.org/10.1016/j.neubiorev.2020.07.006

Bennett, R. (2009). Impulsive donation decisions during online browsing of charity websites. *Journal of Consumer Behavior, 8,* 116–134.

Bennett, R., & Gabriel, H. (1999). Organisational factors and knowledge management within large marketing departments: An empirical study. *Journal of Knowledge Management, 3*(3), 212–225.

Blackbaud Institute. (2015). *Diversity in giving* (pp. 1–16). Charleston, SC: Blackbaud.

Blake, T., Nosko, C., & Tadelis, S. (2015). Consumer heterogeneity and paid search effectiveness: A large-scale field experiment. *Econometrica, 83*(1), 155–174.

Blommel, L. (2017, March 10). The SCLU's new rallying cry: "See you in court, and see you in the streets." *Alternet.* www.alternet.org/news-amp-politics/aclus-new-rallying-cry-see-you-court-and-see-you-streets

Bringle, R., Hedgepath, A., & Wall, E. (2018). "I am so angry I could. . . help!": The nature of empathic anger. *International Journal of Research on Service-Learning and Community Engagement, 6* (1), Article 3.

Brooks, A. (2006). *Who really cares.* New York: Basic Books.

Brown, E., & Ferris, J. (2007). Social capital and philanthropy: An analysis of the impact of social capital on individual giving and volunteering. *Nonprofit and Voluntary Sector Quarterly, 36*(1), 85–99.

Cantrell, D. J. (2019). Love, anger, and social change. *Drexel Law Review, 12,* 47.

Center on Philanthropy at Indiana University. (2010). The 2010 study of high net worth philanthropy: Issues driving charitable activities among affluent households. https://scholarworks.iupui.edu/handle/1805/5666

Chen, Y., Li, X., & MacKie-Mason, J. (2005). Online fund-raising mechanisms: A field experiment. *The BE Journal of Economic Analysis & Policy, 5*(2), 1–37.

CNN. (2010, April 28). Activists call foul on KFC bucket campaign. www.cnn.com/2010/LIVING/homestyle/04/28/kfc.pink.bucket.campaign/index.html

Cole, E., & Stewart, A. (1996). Meanings of political participation among Black and White women: Political identity and social responsibility. *Journal of Personality and Social Psychology, 71*(1), 130–140.

Cole, E. R. (2008). Coalitions as a model for intersectionality: From practice to theory. *Sex Roles, 59*, 443–453.

Coleman, J. (1988). Social capital in the creation of human capital. *American Journal of Sociology, 94*, S95–S120.

Collins, P. (2011). Piecing together a genealogical puzzle: Intersectionality and American pragmatism. *European Journal of Pragmatism and American Philosophy, 3*(III-2), 1–25.

Collinson, S. (2016, November 8). Emotions run high in final days of the campaign. *CNN.* www.cnn.com/2016/11/06/politics/election-2016-emotion-trump-clinton/index.html

Corbet, J. (2020, April 18). Watch: Global citizen hosts "One world: Together at home special to support WHO's COVID-19 response." *Common Dreams.* www.commondreams.org/news/2020/04/18/watch-global-citizen-hosts-one-world-together-home-special-support-whos-covid-19

Corporation for National and Community Service. (2017). *Volunteering and civic life in america.* Bureau of the Census, Washington, DC.

Covin, J., & Slevin, D. (1998). Adherence to plans, risk taking, and environment as predictors of firm growth. *The Journal of High Technology Management Research, 9*(2), 207–237.

Cravens, J. (2014). Internet-mediated volunteering in the EU. *JRC Scientific and Policy Reports.* https://publications.jrc.ec.europa.eu/repository/bit stream/JRC85755/jrc85755.pdf

Crenshaw, K. (1989). Demarginalizing the intersection of race and sex: A black feminist critique of antidiscrimination doctrine, feminist theory and antiracist politics. *University of Chicago Legal Review, 1989*(1), 139–167.

Crenshaw, K. (1991). Mapping the margins: Intersectionality, identity politics, and violence against women of color. *Stanford Law Review, 43*, 1241–1299.

Curtin, N., Stewart, A., & Cole, E. (2015). Challenging the status quo. *Psychology of Women Quarterly, 39*(4), 512–529.

Dawes, C., Loewen, P., & Fowler, J. (2011). Social preferences and political participation. *The Journal of Politics, 73*(3), 845–856.

Deloitte. (2019). The future of wealth in the United States. Retrieved online at https://www2.deloitte.com/content/dam/insights/us/articles/us-generational-wealth-trends/DUP_1371_Future-wealth-in-America_MASTER.pdf. Deloitte University Press, New York.

Deschamps, R., & McNutt, K. (2014). Third sector and social media. *Canadian Journal of Nonprofit and Social Economy Research, 5*(2), 29–46.

Dimock, M. (2019). *Defining generations: Where millennials end and generation Z begins.* Washington, DC: Pew Research Center.

Doolittle, A., & Faul, A. C. (2013). Civic engagement scale: A validation study. *Sage Open, 3*(3), 1–7.

Edlin, A., Gelman, A., & Kaplan, N. (2007). Voting as a rational choice: Why and how people vote to improve the well-being of others. *Rationality and Society, 19*(3), 293–314.

Ellison, N., Steinfield, C., & Lampe, C. (2007). The benefits of Facebook "friends": Social emotion and explanation in protest mobilization. *Social & Cultural Geography, 13*(6), 1143–1168.

Ertas, N. (2016). Millennials and volunteering: Sector differences and implications for public service motivation theory. *Public Administration Quarterly, 40*(3), 517–558.

Feng, Y., Du, L., & Ling, Q. (2017). How social media strategies of nonprofit organizations affect consumer donation intention and word-of-mouth. *Social Behavior and Personality: An International Journal, 45*(11), 1775–1786.

Ferry, A. (2017, September 29). Episodic giving and the rise of "rage donation". *Medium.* https://medium.com/galaxy-digital/episodic-giving-and-the-rise-of-the-ragedonationd13b5a422fb1

File, T. (2017, May 10). Voting in America: A look at the 2016 presidential election. *Bureau of the Census,* Washington DC. www.census.gov/news room/blogs/random-samplings/2017/05/voting_in_america.html

Flanagan, C. (2003). Developmental roots of political engagement. *PS: Political Science & Politics, 36*(2), 257–261.

Ford, B. Q., Feinberg, M., Lam, P., Mauss, I. B., & John, O. P. (2019). Using reappraisal to regulate negative emotion after the 2016 U.S. presidential election: Does emotion regulation Trump political action? *Journal of Personality and Social Psychology, 117*(5), 998–1015.

Fowler, J., & Kam, C. (2007). Beyond the self: Social identity, altruism, and political participation. *The Journal of Politics, 69*(3), 813–827.

Galston, W. A. (2017, July 31). Millennials will soon be the largest voting bloc in America. *The Brookings Institute.* www.brookings.edu/blog/fixgov/2017/07/31/millennials-will-soon-be-the-largest-voting-bloc-in-america/

Gálvez-Rodriguez, M., Caba-Pérez, C., & López-Godoy, M. (2014). Facebook: A new communication strategy for non-profit organisations in Colombia. *Public Relations Review, 40*(5), 868–870.

Gamson, W., & Meyer, D. (1996). Framing political opportunity. In D. McAdam, J. McCarthy, & M. Zald (Eds.), *Comparative perspectives on social movements: Political opportunities, mobilizing structures, and cultural framings* (pp. 275–290). Cambridge: Cambridge University Press.

Gilbert, P. (2017). Compassion as a social mentality: An evolutionary approach. In P. Gilbert (Ed.), *Compassion: Concepts, research and applications* (pp. 31–68). Routledge/Taylor & Francis Group.

Gines, K. (2014). Race women, race men and early expressions of proto-intersectionality, 1830s–1930s. In N. Goswami, M. M. O'Donovan, & L. Yount (Eds.), *Why race and gender still matter: An intersectional approach* (pp. 13–26). New York: Routledge.

Giving USA. (2019, June 18). Giving USA: The annual report on philanthropy for the year 2018. *Giving USA Foundation, Indiana University Lilly Family School of Philanthropy.* www.givingusa.org

Goldseker, S., & Moody, M. (2017). Show me the impact. *Stanford Social Innovation Review.* https://doi.org/10.48558/Z144-QM8

Gorczyca, M., & Hartman, R. (2017). The new face of philanthropy: The role of intrinsic motivation in millennials' attitudes and intent to donate to charitable organizations. *Journal of Nonprofit and Public Sector Marketing, 29*(4), 415–433.

Graham, C., & Pinto, S. (2017, February 2). The Trump. *Brookings.* www.brookings.edu/blog/up-front/2017/02/02/the-trump-unhappiness-effect-nears-the-great-recession-for-many/

Grant, A. (2008). Employees without a cause: The motivational effects of prosocial impact in public service. *International Public Management Journal, 11*(1), 48–66.

Green, T., & Tyson, A. (2020, April 2). 5 facts about partisan reactions to COVID-19 in the U.S. *Pew Research Center.* www.pewresearch.org/fact-tank/2020/04/02/5-facts-about-partisan-reactions-to-covid-19-in-the-u-s/

Greenaway, K., Cichocka, A., van Veelen, R., Likki, T., & Branscombe, N. (2016). Feeling hopeful inspires support for social change. *Political Psychology, 37*(1), 89–107.

Greenwood, R. (2008). Intersectional political consciousness: Appreciation for intragroup differences and solidarity in diverse groups. *Psychology of Women Quarterly, 32*(1), 36–47.

Groenendyk, E., & Banks, A. (2014). Emotional rescue: How affect helps partisans overcome collective action problems. *Political Psychology, 35*(3), 359–378.

Grootaert, C., Narayan, D., Jones, V., & Woolcock, M. (2004). *Measuring social capital: An integrated questionnaire. World Bank Working Paper; No. 18.* World Bank, Washington, DC. https://openknowledge.worldbank.org/handle/10986/15033

Guidry, J., Jin, Y., Orr, C., Messner, M., & Meganck, S. (2017). Ebola on Instagram and Twitter: How health organizations address the health crisis in their social media engagement. *Public Relations Review*, *43*(3), 477–486.

Guo, C., & Saxton, G. (2014). Tweeting social change: How social media are changing nonprofit advocacy. *Nonprofit and Voluntary Sector Quarterly*, *43* (1), 57–79.

Guynn, J. (2018, June 20). "Rage giving" fuels record fundraising for immigrant children: "Every time I get mad, I do it again." *USA Today*. www .usatoday.com/story/tech/2018/06/20/rage-giving-fuels-record-fundraising-immigrant-children/718272002/

Harnett, B. & Matan, R. (2014). Generational differences in philanthropic giving. Nonprofit and Social Services Group. Fall 2014. Sobel & Co., LLC.

Harvard, E. (2019). Motivations for charitable giving among generations X and Y: Applying an extended theory of planned behavior to independent school alumni. *University of Richmond, School of Professional and Continuing Studies Nonprofit Studies Capstone Project*. https://scholarship.richmond .edu/spcs-nonprofitstudies-capstones/7

Haryani, S., & Motwani, B. (2015). Discriminant model for online viral marketing influencing consumers behavioural intention. *Pacific Science Review B: Humanities and Social Sciences*, *1*(1), 49–56.

Helm, S. (2010). Viral marketing: Establishing customer relationships by "word-of-mouse." *Electronic Commerce and Marketing*, *10*(3), 158–161.

Hinde, R. A., & Groebel, J. (Eds.). (1991). *Cooperation and prosocial behaviour*. New York: Cambridge University Press.

Hodges, J. (2018, December 12). Why you shouldn't donate angry: Pitfalls of rage giving. *Yes! Solutions Journalism*. www.yesmagazine.org/social-justice /2018/12/12/why-being-angry-is-all-the-rage-in-charitable-giving/

Hoffman, M. (2010). Empathy and prosocial behavior. In M. Lewis, J. Haviland-Jones, & L. Barrett (Eds.), *Handbook of emotions* (3rd ed.) (pp. 440–455). New York: Guilford Press.

Hull, C., & Lio, B. (2006). Innovation in non-profit and for-profit organizations: Visionary, strategic, and financial considerations. *Journal of Change Management*, *6*(1), 53–65.

Hyman, J. (2002). Exploring social capital and civic engagement to create a framework for community building. *Applied Developmental Sciences*, *6*(4), 196–202.

Icha, O., & Agwu, E. (2015). Effectiveness of social media networks as a strategic tool for organizational marketing management. *Journal of Internet Banking Commerce*, S2(6), 1–9.

Ihm, J. (2017). Classifying and relating different types of online and offline volunteering. *Voluntas: International Journal of Voluntary and Nonprofit Organizations, 28*(1), 400–419.

IUPUI Women's Philanthropy Institute. (2019). *Women give 2019: Gender and giving across communities of color* (pp. 1–44). Indianapolis, IN: Indiana University.

Jankowski, R. (2002). Buying a lottery ticket to help the poor: Altruism, civic duty, and self-interest in the decision to vote. *Rationality and Society, 14*(1), 55–77.

Jankowski, R. (2007). Altruism and the decision to vote: Explaining and testing high voter turnout. *Rationality and Society, 19*(1), 5–34.

Kietzmann, J., Hermkens, K., McCarthy, I., & Silvestre, B. (2011). Social media? Get serious! Understanding the functional building blocks of social media. *Business Horizons, 54*(3), 241–251.

Kupperschmidt, B. R. (2000). Multi-generation employees: Strategies for effective management. *Health Care Manager, 19*(1), 65–76.

Lacetera, N., Macis, M., & Mele, A. (2014). Viral altruism? Generosity and social contagion in online networks. *Sociological Science, 3*(11), 202–238. http://dx.doi.org/10.15195/v3.a11

Lai, C. H., She, B., & Tao, C. C. (2017). Connecting the dots: A longitudinal observation of relief organizations' representational networks on social media. *Computers in Human Behavior, 74*, 224–234.

Langstraat, L., & Bowdon, M. (2011). Service-learning and critical emotion studies: On the perils of empathy and the politics of compassion. *Michigan Journal of Community Service Learning, 17*(2), 5–14.

Lee, B. (2020, April 19). "One world: Together at home" convers: Start support COVID-19 coronavirus efforts. *Forbes.* www.forbes.com/sites/brucelee/2020/04/19/one-world-together-at-home-concert-stars-support-covid-19-coronavirus-efforts/#434ea5a1a0d7

Lee, M. (2018). Behavioral analysis of rage donating from 2014 through the 2016 presidential election (Unpublished thesis). Colorado College, Colorado Springs.

Lee, Y., & Chang, C. (2007). Who gives what to charity? Characteristics affecting donation behavior. *Social Behavior and Personality: An International Journal, 35*(9), 1173–1180.

Leroux, K., & Goerdel, H. T. (2009). Political advocacy by nonprofit organizations: A strategic management explanation. *Public Performance & Management Review, 32*(4), 514–536.

Lewis, R., & Reiley, D. (2014). Online ads and offline sales: Measuring the effect of re- tail advertising via a controlled experiment on Yahoo! *Quantitative Marketing and Economics, 12*(3), 235–266.

Lewis, R. A., & Rao, J. M. (2015). The unfavorable economics of measuring the returns to advertising. *The Quarterly Journal of Economics, 130*(4), 1941–1973.

Linden, W., Hogan, B. E., Rutledge, T. et al. (2003). There is more to anger coping than "in" or "out". *Emotion, 3*(1), 12.

Lyman, P. (2004). The domestication of anger. *European Journal of Social Theory, 7*(2), 133–147.

MacLaughlin, S. (2017, August 23). Understanding the rage-donation: How to engage beyond the episodic gift. *NPEngage.* npengage.com/nonprofit-fundraising/rage-donation/

Markus, H. R., & Kitayama, S. (1991). Culture and the self: Implications for cognition, emotion, and motivation. *Psychological Review, 98*(2), 224.

Mayer, S. (2020). Can we make use of all this anger? An analysis of rage donation after the 2016 election (Unpublished thesis). Colorado College, Colorado Springs.

McDonald, M. P. (2020, December 7). United States Elections Project. *Elect Project.* www.electproject.org/

McHugh, M. (2018, June 22). Rage giving: The productive side of social media outrage. *The Ringer.* www.theringer.com/tech/2018/6/22/17494052/rage-giving-trump-immigration-twitter

Mettler, K. (2016, November 15). People are donating to planned parenthood in Mike Pence's name, *The Washington Post.* www.washingtonpost.com/news/morning-mix/wp/2016/11/15/people-are-donating-to-planned-parenthood-in-mike-pences-name/?utm_term=.4e2ba2ef2bb9

Micciche, L. (2007). *Doing emotion: Rhetoric, writing, teaching.* Portsmouth: Boynton/Cook.

Miers, A., Rieffe, C., Meerum Terwogt, M., Cowan, R., & Linden, W. (2007). The relation between anger coping strategies, anger mood and somatic complaints in children and adolescents. *Journal of Abnormal Child Psychology, 35*, 653–664.

Miller, D. (1983). The correlates of entrepreneurship in three types of firms. *Management Science, 29*(7), 770–791.

Nah, S., & Saxton, G. (2013). Modeling the adoption and use of social media by nonprofit organizations. *New Media & Society, 15*(2), 294–313.

Namisango, F., & Kang, K. (2018). Social media, organisation-community relationships and co-creation: A case of nonprofit organizations. *Association for Information Systems, Research Presented at the 24th Americas Conference on Information Systems, New Orleans.*

Network of Schools of Public Policy, Affairs, and Administration. (n.d.). Standards and guidance. www.naspaa.org/accreditation/standards-and-guidance

Nicolaou, E., & Smith, C. (2019, October 5). A #MeToo timeline to show how far we've come – & how far we need to go. *Refinery 29.* www.refinery29.com /en-us/2018/10/212801/me-too-movement-history-timeline-year-weinstein

Nonprofit Academic Centers Council. (2019, July 1). NACC curricular guidelines, revised, 2019. www.nonprofit-academic-centers-council.org/curricu lar-guidelines/

Nonprofit Source. (2018, May 1). 2018 online giving statistics, trends & data: The ultimate list of giving stats. https://nonprofitssource.com/online-giving-statistics/

Nonprofit Technology Network. (2012, April 27). Nonprofit social network benchmark report. https://www.nten.org/NTEN_images/reports/2012_non profit_social_networking_benchmark_report_final.pdf

Nussbaum, M. C. (2001). *Upheavals of thought: The intelligence of emotions.* Cambridge: Cambridge University Press.

Ost, D. (2004). Politics as the mobilization of anger: Emotions in movements and in power. *European Journal of Social Theory, 7*(2), 229–244.

Paulin, M., Ferguson, R., Schattke, K., & Jost, N. (2014). Millennials, social media, prosocial emotions, and charitable causes: The paradox of gender differences. *Journal of Nonprofit & Public Sector Marketing, 26,* 335–353.

Payton, R. (1988). *Philanthropy: Voluntary action for the public good.* New York: American Council on Education/Macmillan.

Peng, L. (2017). Crisis crowdsourcing and China's civic participation in disaster response: Evidence from earthquake relief. *China Information, 31*(3), 327–348.

Perry, J., Hondeghem, A., & Wise, L. (2010). Revisiting the motivational bases of public service: Twenty years of research and an agenda for the future. *Public Administration Review, 70*(5), 682–690.

Pew Research Center. (2015). *America's changing religious landscape.* Washington, DC.

Piper, K. (2019, July 20). The ice bucket challenge and the promise – and the pitfalls – of viral charity. *Vox.* www.vox.com/future-perfect/2019/7/20/ 20699732/ice-bucket-challenge-viral-charity-als

Plutchik, R. (2001). The nature of emotions: Human emotions have deep evolutionary roots, a fact that may explain their complexity and provide tools for clinical practice. *American Scientist, 89*(4), 344–350.

Pope, J., Sterrett, I., & Asamoa-Tutu, F. (2009). Developing a marketing strategy for nonprofit organizations: An exploratory study. *Journal of Nonprofit and Public Sector Marketing, 21*(2), 184–201.

Prahalad, C. K., & Ramaswamy, V. (2004). Co-creation experiences: The next practice in value creation. *Journal of Interactive Marketing, 18*(3), 5–14.

Putnam, R. (1995, January). The strange disappearance of civic America. *The American Prospect*. http://prospect.org/article/strange-disappearance-civic-america

Putnam, R. (2000). *Bowling alone: The collapse and revival of American community*. New York: Simon & Schuster.

Putnam, R. (2002). Bowling together: The United State of America. *The American Prospect, 13*(Feb. 11), 20–22.

Rage Donate. (2017). #RageAgainstHate. www.ragedonate.com/

Rainey, H., & Steinbauer, P. (1999). Galloping elephants: Developing elements of a theory of effective government organizations. *Journal of Public Administration Research and Theory, 9*(1), 1–32. https://wiredimpact.com/blog/rage-donations-nonprofit-trend/

Ramaswamy, V., & Ozcan, K. (2014). *The co-creation paradigm*. Stanford: Stanford University Press.

Rathi, D., Given, L., & Forcier, E. (2016). Knowledge needs in the non-profit sector: An evidence-based model of organizational practices. *Journal of Knowledge Management, 20*(1), 23–48.

Rinkunas, S. (2016, December 26). Planned parenthood received 40 times its usual number of donations after the election. *The Cut* www.thecut.com/2016/12/planned-parenthood-donations-are-up-40-fold-since-election.html

Robinson, C. C. (2019). (Re) theorizing civic engagement: Foundations for Black Americans civic engagement theory. *Sociology Compass, 13*(9), e12728.

Romero, A., & Rozanski, G. (2017). A revamped ACLU takes on today's fights. *Stanford Social Innovation Review, 15*(3), 25–31.

Sargeant, A., Ford, J., & West, D. (2006). Perceptual determinants of nonprofit giving behavior. *Journal of Business Research, 59*(2), 155–165. https://doi.org/10.1016/j.jbusres.2005.04.006.

Saxton, G., Guo, S., & Brown, W. (2007). New dimensions of nonprofit responsiveness: The application and promise of Internet-based technologies. *Public Performance & Management Review, 31*(2), 144–173.

Scherer, K. (2005). What are emotions? And how can they be measured? *Social Science Information, 44*(4), 695–729.

Schmid, H., Bar, M., & Nirel, R. (2008). Advocacy activities in nonprofit human service organizations. *Nonprofit and Voluntary Sector Quarterly, 37*(4), 581–602.

Seaquist, C. (2017, February 15). The anger election of 2016: How will we handle our anger? *Huffington Post*. www.huffpost.com/entry/the-anger-election-of-201_b_9234334

Segedin, A. (2018, April 11). Rage giving fueled uptick in 2017 fundraising. *The Nonprofit Times.* www.thenonprofittimes.com/news-articles/rage-giving-fueled-uptick-2017-fundraising/

Silber, I. (2012). The angry gift: A neglected facet of philanthropy. *Current Sociology, 60*(3), 320–337.

Smith, A., & Anderson, M. (2018, March 1). Social media use in 2018 (Rep.). *Pew Research Center.* www.pewinternet.org/2018/03/01/social-media-use-in-2018

Sorensen, A., Andrews, L., & Drennan, J. (2017). Using social media posts as resources for engaging in value co-creation: The case for social media-based cause brand communities. *Journal of Service Theory and Practice, 27*(4), 898–922.

Statistics on U.S. Generosity. (2015). The Philanthropy Roundtable. https://www.philanthropyroundtable.org/resource/statistics-on-u-s-generosity/

Suh, J. (2020). Revenue sources matter to nonprofit communication? An examination of museum communication and social media engagement. *Journal of Nonprofit & Public Sector Marketing,* 1–20.

Swift, A. (2016, July 21). Americans' satisfaction with U.S. drops sharply. *Gallup.* http://news.gallup.com/poll/193832/americans-satisfaction-drops-sharply.aspx

Tanksley, T. (2019). *Race, education and #BlackLivesMatter: How social media activism shapes the educational experiences of Black college-age women* (Doctoral dissertation). University of California, Los Angeles.

Taylor, J., Miller-Stevens, K., Baker, J., & Lee, M. (2018). Armchair resistance: Rage giving and civic engagement. *Research Presented at the National Conference of the Association for Research on Nonprofit Organizations and Voluntary Action, Austin, Texas.*

Taylor, J., & Noble, S. (2015). Ice, ice, maybe? Determinants of viral fundraising. *Research Presented at the 43rd Annual Conference of the Association of Research on Nonprofit and Voluntary Organizations,* Denver, Colorado.

Teson, K. (2017, April 12). Rage donations: Is your nonprofit ready for this new trend? *Wired Impact.* https://wiredimpact.com/blog/rage-donations-nonprofit-trend

Thackeray, R., Neiger, B., Smith, A., & Van Wagenen, S. (2012). Adoption and use of social media among public health departments. *BMC Public Health, 12*(1), 242.

Thaler, R. (1985). Mental accounting and consumer choice. *Marketing Science, 4*(3), 199–214.

Treiblmaier, H., & Pollach, I. (2006). A framework for measuring people's intention to donate online. *Tenth Pacific Asia Conference on Information Systems (PAIC)*, 808–819.

Tropp, L., & Uluğ, Ö. (2019). Are white women showing up for racial justice? Intergroup contact, closeness to people targeted by prejudice, and collective action. *Psychology of Women Quarterly, 43*(3), 335–347.

US Department of Commerce. (2019). Quarterly retail e-commerce sales. Press release dated May 19, 2020. www.census.gov/retail/mrts/www/data/pdf/ec_current.pdf

Uluğ, Ö., & Cohrs, J. (2017). "If we become friends, maybe I can change my perspective": Intergroup contact, endorsement of conflict narratives and peace-related attitudes in Turkey. *Peace and Conflict: Journal of Peace Psychology, 23*, 278–287.

Valentino, N., Brader, T., Groenendyk, E., Gregorowicz, K., & Hutchings, V. (2011). Election night's alright for fighting: The role of emotions in political participation. *The Journal of Politics, 73*(1), 156–170.

Valentino, N. A., Wayne, C., & Oceno, M. (2018). Mobilizing sexism: The interaction of emotion and gender attitudes in the 2016 US presidential election. *Public Opinion Quarterly, 82*(S1), 799–821.

Valenzuela, S., Park, N., & Kee, K. (2009). Is there social capital in a social network site? Facebook use and college students' life satisfaction, trust, and participation. *Journal of Computer-Mediated Communication, 14*(4), 875–901.

Venkatesh, S. (2002). Race and philanthropy: An introduction. *Souls, 4*(1), 32–34.

Vitaglione, G., & Barnett, M. (2003). Assessing a new dimension of empathy: Empathic anger as a predictor of helping and punishing desires. *Motivation and Emotion, 27*(4), 301–325.

von Salisch, M., & Vogelgesang, J. (2005). Anger regulation among friends: Assessment and development from childhood to adolescence. *Journal of Social and Personal Relationships, 22*(6), 837–855.

Waasdorp, E. (2018, July 9). 3 crucial steps to converting rage donors to long-term supporters (and 3 bonus steps). *NonProfitPRO*. www.nonprofitpro.com/post/3-crucial-steps-to-converting-rage-donors-to-long-term-supporters-and-3-bonus-steps/

Ward, K. D., & Miller-Stevens, K. (2021. Public service motivation among nonprofit board members and the influence of primary sector of employment. *Nonprofit and Voluntary Sector Quarterly, 50*(2), 312–334. http://doi.org/0899764020952161

Warner, T., Abel, A., & Hachtmann, F. (2014). Empowered and engaged: Exploring social media best practices for nonprofits. *Journal of Digital & Social Media Marketing, 1*(4), 391–403.

Waters, R., Burnett, E., Lamm, A., & Lucas, J. (2009). Engaging stakeholders through social networking: How nonprofit organizations are using Facebook. *Public Relations Review, 35*, 102–106.

Watkins, E. (2004). Appraisals and strategies associated with rumination and worry. *Personality and Individual Differences, 37*(4), 679–694.

WealthEngine. (2019, May 29). A look at millennial wealth. https://go.wealthengine.com/millennial-wealth-2019.

Williams, A., & Taylor, J. (2013). Resolving accountability ambiguity in nonprofit organizations. *Voluntas: International Journal of Voluntary and Nonprofit Organizations, 24*(3), 559–580.

Winans, A. (2012). Cultivating critical emotional literacy: Cognitive and contemplative approaches to engaging difference. *College English, 75*(2), 150–170.

Woods, M., Anderson, J., Guilbert, S., & Watkin, S. (2012). "The country (side) is angry": Emotion and explanation in protest mobilization. *Social & Cultural Geography, 13*(6), 567–585.

Wray-Lake, L., DeHaan, C. R., Shubert, J., & Ryan, R. M. (2019). Examining links from civic engagement to daily well-being from a self-determination theory perspective. *The Journal of Positive Psychology, 14*(2), 166–177.

Wyllie, J., Lucas, B., Kitchens, B. et al. (2016, February 22). A small-scale analysis of health service stakeholder networks: Insights from social media. *Cambridge Service Alliance, University of Cambridge.* https://cambridgeservicealliance.eng.cam.ac.uk/resources/Downloads/Monthly%20Papers/2016FebPaper_AnalysisofHealthServiceStakeholderNetworks.pdf

Yörük, B. K. (2009). How responsive are charitable donors to requests to give?. *Journal of Public Economics, 93*(9–10), 1111–1117.

Yao, K. (2015). Who gives? The determinants of charitable giving, volunteering, and their relationship. *Wharton Research Scholars, 126*, 1–34.

Yen, S. (2002). An econometric analysis of household donations in the USA. *Applied Economics Letters, 9*, 837–841.

Young, J. (2017). Facebook, Twitter, and blogs: The adoption and utilization of social media in nonprofit human service organizations. *Human Service Organizations: Management, Leadership & Governance, 41*(11), 44–57.

Cambridge Elements ≡

Public and Nonprofit Administration

Andrew Whitford
University of Georgia

Andrew Whitford is Alexander M. Crenshaw Professor of Public Policy in the School of Public and International Affairs at the University of Georgia. His research centers on strategy and innovation in public policy and organization studies.

Robert Christensen
Brigham Young University

Robert Christensen is professor and George Romney Research Fellow in the Marriott School at Brigham Young University. His research focuses on prosocial and antisocial behaviors and attitudes in public and nonprofit organizations.

About the Series

The foundation of this series are cutting-edge contributions on emerging topics and definitive reviews of keystone topics in public and nonprofit administration, especially those that lack longer treatment in textbook or other formats. Among keystone topics of interest for scholars and practitioners of public and nonprofit administration, it covers public management, public budgeting and finance, nonprofit studies, and the interstitial space between the public and nonprofit sectors, along with theoretical and methodological contributions, including quantitative, qualitative and mixed-methods pieces.

The Public Management Research Association

The Public Management Research Association improves public governance by advancing research on public organizations, strengthening links among interdisciplinary scholars, and furthering professional and academic opportunities in public management.

Cambridge Elements ⁼

Public and Nonprofit Administration

Elements in the Series

A full series listing is available at: www.cambridge.org/EPNP

Printed in the United States
by Baker & Taylor Publisher Services